Police Research Series
Paper 150

Drunks and Disorder: Processing intoxicated arrestees in two city-centre custody suites

Ann Deehan
Emma Marshall
Esther Saville

"The views expressed in this report are those of the authors, not necessarily those of the Home Office (nor do they reflect Government policy)."

Editor: Lawrence Singer
Home Office
Policing and Reducing Crime Unit
Research, Development and Statistics Directorate
Clive House, Petty France
London, SW1H 9HD

Policing and Reducing Crime Unit: Police Research Series

The Policing and Reducing Crime Unit (PRC Unit) is part of the Research, Development and Statistics Directorate of the Home Office. The PRC Unit carries out and commissions research in the social and management sciences on policing and crime reduction.

The Police Research Series presents research material on crime prevention and detection as well as police management and organisation issues.

ISBN 1-84082-788-2

Copies of this publication can be made available in formats accessible to the visually impaired on request.

Foreword

For many people, the consumption of alcohol is an integral part of night-time entertainment and is enjoyed without incident. However, in late night city-centre entertainment districts the public order problems presented by a significant minority of intoxicated people are all too evident, especially at the weekends. These have become of prime concern to both licensees and the police. For the police, intoxicated arrestees present special management difficulties when brought into custody, not least because they are at heightened risk of dying whilst in police custody. The nature and extent of these difficulties raise questions about alternative arrangements for the care and detention of intoxicated arrestees.

This exploratory study demonstrates that a disproportionate number of arrestees brought into city-centre custody suites late at night are intoxicated and charged with assault, public disorder offences and drink-driving. Furthermore, it provides graphic illustrations of the problems associated with drunken arrestees in custody, such as aggressive behaviour, non-compliance, and care and hygiene issues, all of which place an additional burden on custody staff. The report concludes by discussing the potential for the provision of public health interventions, as well as the possibility of alternative specialist centres to hold and care for drunken detainees.

Lawrence Singer
Head of Policing Group
Policing and Reducing Crime Unit
Research, Development and Statistics Directorate
Home Office
January 2002

Acknowledgements

Thanks are due to all members of the police service and the licensees who participated in this study and were so generous with their time and expertise. In addition we would like to thank Louisa Bullock and Nerys Thomas from the Policing and Reducing Crime Unit who undertook some of the fieldwork for the study. Thanks also go to Cressy Bridgeman for her comments and support throughout the project, and Tracey Budd and Andrea Finney for their help in preparing the report for publication.

The authors

At the time of the research Ann Deehan was a Senior Research Officer in the Policing and Reducing Crime Unit where Emma Marshall and Esther Saville were Research Officers. Ann Deehan has since moved to the National Centre for Education and Training on Addiction, Flinders University of Australia, Adelaide; Emma Marshall is working in the Neighbourhood Renewal Unit at the Department for Transport Local Government and the Regions; and Esther Saville is a Research Fellow at the Centre for Drug Misuse Research, University of Glasgow.

The Policing and Reducing Crime Unit would like to thank Professor Mike Maguire of the School of Social Science, University of Cardiff and Stuart Lister, Centre for Criminal Justice Studies, University of Leeds who acted as external assessors for this report.

Executive summary

This report presents the findings from a research study exploring the problems encountered in policing city-centre entertainment districts and in dealing with intoxicated arrestees in police custody. The report discusses how the police, licensees and partner agencies can work together and, through an holistic and integrated approach, reduce alcohol-related disorder and violence in entertainment areas. It also identifies a number of approaches that could help alleviate the problems presented by drunken detainees in police custody.

Key recommendations

Key recommendations for potential action fall into three categories: city-centre management, deterrence and detection, and care and management in the city-centre.

City-centre management

- strengthening links, with the support of *local partnerships*, between the *various agencies* and *stakeholders* to foster relations and share intelligence and ultimately increase the success of local initiatives

- encouraging the staggering of closing times of entertainment venues, ensuring sufficient fast-food outlets are open and providing adequate transport facilities out of the city-centre to reduce the potential for 'flash-points' outside venues and around fast-food outlets and taxi-ranks.

Deterrence and detection

- targeting resources and deployment of officers to enable high visibility *policing* at identified 'hotspots' at busy times, and the use of CCTV to assist the swift and appropriate deployment of officers

- carefully targeting visits to licensed premises by *local licensing units* at busy times to ensure that laws are not being flouted, and encourage good serving and security practices

- substitution of standard quality glass and bottles with toughened glass or plastic 'glasses' by *licensees*, the 'designing out' of overcrowding in venue layout and implementation of well-advertised good serving and security practices to reduce the potential for incidents to arise or escalate

- installation of well-managed CCTV by licensees, ensuring bar and door staff are well-trained, employing good record-keeping practices, and signing up to Pub Watch and Club Watch schemes to support the 'policing' of the city-centre.

Care and management in the custody suite
- the installation and monitoring of closed circuit cameras in cells containing vulnerable detainees to enable better observation of those at risk of injury or death including those who are intoxicated

- having medically trained staff, whether police, civilian or health professionals, in the custody suite to take responsibility for the health and well-being of arrestees

- screening of arrestees for alcohol problems with consequent referral to external services or the administration of brief intervention in the custody suite as appropriate to reduce future hazardous drinking behaviour

- providing alternative settings for the specialist care and detention of intoxicated arrestees.

Key findings

Problems in entertainment areas

Police and licensees interviewed at both sites reported that drunken people posed problems in their city-centre. They felt that alcohol contributed to nuisance crime, rather than serious violent crime, although they believed that alcohol had the potential to escalate an otherwise minor disagreement into a more serious incident. The police distinguished between the 'habitual drunks' who tended to be arrested in the daytime and came into contact with the police frequently for petty crime; and the weekend 'binge drinkers' who consumed large amounts of alcohol in single drinking sessions, were less likely to have previous contact with the police but were more likely to be violent or disorderly.

The police were concerned with public disorder on the streets and the need to ensure the safety of the public. Officers routinely reasoned with potential arrestees in order to try to avoid the need for arrest. Key factors that informed the decision to arrest included the offenders' physical vulnerability, the potential for violence, and the likelihood that the individual will commit a further offence.

Problems presented by intoxicated arrestees in police custody

About three-quarters of the 169 arrestees observed during the fieldwork period admitted to custody staff that they had consumed alcohol prior to arrest and 59 per cent were classified as being intoxicated (either based on the amount they admitted consuming or observed behavioural or physical signs of intoxication). Almost 60 per cent of intoxicated arrestees were arrested for alcohol-specific offences, such as being drunk and disorderly or drink-driving. A fifth (20%) were arrested for public order offences and a further 12 per cent for assault. Intoxicated arrestees were more likely to be arrested after midnight and on the street than non-intoxicated arrestees.

Processing and custody time

In general, intoxicated arrestees took less time to process into custody than those not intoxicated (often because they were put into the cells more quickly due to their condition) and were on average held in custody for less time. However, for public order offences and assault, intoxicated arrestees were held in custody for three to five times longer than their non-intoxicated counterparts, partly because they could not be interviewed until they had sobered up.

Medical assistance

Intoxicated arrestees place a particular responsibility on custody sergeants who have to decide whether the arrestee requires a visit from a Forensic Medical Examiner (FME) or needs to be sent directly to an Accident and Emergency Department.

The FME assesses fitness to be detained and potential for self-harm and deals with any injury or illness. This research indicates that the majority of the work of FMEs involves intoxicated detainees. 73 per cent of arrestees attended by an FME were considered to be intoxicated. If FMEs consider an arrestee fit to be detained they will usually request frequent checks – sometimes as often as every 15 minutes – by custody staff to ensure the well-being of the detainee.

Non compliance and aggression

Intoxicated arrestees were far more likely to display signs of non-compliance and aggression during processing into custody than those who were not intoxicated. 31 per cent of intoxicated arrestees were judged as non-compliant or only partially compliant; 42 per cent displayed aggression. The figures for non-intoxicated arrestees were five per cent and eight per cent respectively. Aggression most often took the form of verbal abuse, though 14 per cent of intoxicated arrestees used physical force.

Other issues

Intoxicated arrestees are particularly likely to present hygiene problems for custody staff – urinating or defecating in their clothing during or after arrest. They can also be disruptive, for example being noisy whilst being held in cells. A particular problem was the need for a female officer to be in attendance during certain procedures with female arrestees, for example when the FME attended. This required female officers to be taken from other duties.

Related research

The reader is referred to a related research study commissioned by the Home Office that explores the role of Forensic Medical Examiners and their attitudes towards providing a brief health intervention to drunken detainees. The study further adds to our knowledge about the problems encountered in the criminal justice system when dealing with drunken offenders and the feasibility of alternative approaches. The results are published in *The role of the forensic medical examiner with 'drunken detainees' in police custody*, Police Research Series Paper 146.

Methodological note

Two sites in metropolitan areas with late-night entertainment areas were studied. Observational research was carried out in both sites between 10.30pm and 3.30am to coincide with the main pub and club closing times, and covered two weekday periods (Monday to Thursday) and two weekend periods (Friday to Sunday) at each site. The research included the collection of standardised information on each of the 169 individuals brought into custody during the research period and detailed observational field notes, taken as events unfolded. In addition, 31 semi-structured interviews were undertaken with police officers, civilian jailers, licensing officers and local licensees at the sites.

Although the research is based on custody suites located in city-centre entertainment areas and does not purport to present a nationally representative picture across all custody suites, the problems identified are likely to be experienced widely.

Contents

List of tables and boxes

1. Introduction

Background

The role of alcohol in crime is not clear. It is estimated that 22 per cent of arrestees test positive for alcohol and those with alcohol in their system are most likely to have been arrested for disorder offences (Bennett, 2000). The actual proportion could be higher in reality as the Bennett study, based on a small geographically confined sample[1], excluded those arrestees who were thought to be too drunk to interview. The British Crime Survey (Kershaw et al., 2000) also provides some evidence of a link between alcohol and violent crime: 40 per cent of victims of violent crime thought that their assailant was under the influence of alcohol and over 53 per cent of stranger violent attacks occurred in or near pubs and clubs. Drinking in bars has been shown to be more strongly associated with violent or aggressive behaviour than drinking in other settings (see for example, Homel et al., 1991; Stockwell et al., 1993), and there is evidence that many of the incidents of violence and disorder in or around licensed establishments occur at weekends (Marsh and Fox Kibby, 1992).

1 *Sample size was 500 arrestees over four sites.*

The available literature commonly describes alcohol-related crimes as being incidents that:

- involve a combination of criminal damage offences, drunk and disorderly offences and other public order offences

- involve young males between the ages of 18 and 30 years

- occur in a very small, segmented entertainment area of city or town centres.

However, there has been no research on the problems that drunken offenders potentially create for the police once in custody. This study was undertaken to gain insight into these problems. The study recorded numbers of arrests made, reason for arrest, characteristics of the arrestees and evidence of intoxication. In addition, observational data was collected on the behaviour of arrested individuals, with a particular focus on displays of aggression and non-compliance with the custody process.

Methodology

Choosing a method to research issues such as these is difficult for many reasons. Existing data sources such as custody records provide much information about offenders arrested for specific drunkenness offences, such as drunk and disorderly or drink-driving, but do not necessarily identify drunken offenders arrested for other types of offence, such as assault. Furthermore, retrospective data collection based on custody records would not describe the difficulties experienced in the custody suite and the context within which interactions take place. For this reason, this study employed a combination of research techniques, including observation in custody suites and semi-structured interviews with the police and licensees.

Observational research

There have been a number of studies conducted in police custody suites which have focused upon police procedures, professional conduct and behaviour (for example, Softley, 1980; Phillips and Brown, 1998). This study examines the behaviour of the arrestee in custody and the implications for the arresting officers and custody staff involved in processing and detaining offenders.

It was important that the research did not interfere with the custody process, and as a result it was not possible to gain informed consent from the arrestees under observation. Furthermore, the 1997 Police and Criminal Evidence Act makes all field notes recorded in the custody suite open to disclosure in criminal proceedings, potentially making researchers appear to police officers as 'spies in the camp' (Phillips and Brown, 1997). Such research also exposes the researchers to police culture, which could potentially result in less objective data collection and interpretation if, for example, the researcher had particular sympathy with one of the parties being observed. In addition it should be remembered that this research observed only what occurred in the custody suite. Interactions between police officers and arrestees during arrest and prior to arrival in the custody suite were not observed by the researchers. It is likely that in some cases these interactions affected what occurred later in custody (Phillips and Brown, 1998).

The study

Two sites were chosen for study, selected on the basis of size (throughput of at least 600 arrestees per month) and type of area policed – both covered metropolitan areas with large and geographically distinct city-centre entertainment areas. A detailed description of the sites appears at the end of this section.

Observational research was carried out at both sites between November 1999 and February 2000. At both sites four periods of fieldwork were undertaken covering two weekday periods (Monday through to Thursday) and two weekend periods (Friday through to Sunday). Two researchers conducted the observational work between the hours of 10.30pm and 3.30am, coinciding with the main pub and club closing times, to maximise the number of drunken detainees observed.

Two data collection methods were used on site – a data collection schedule designed to provide information on each individual brought into custody during the research period and detailed observational field notes, taken as events unfolded. One researcher collected data on the schedule while the other took detailed field notes. To ensure confidentiality, each individual under observation was given an identification number in the field notes to correspond with a number on the data collection schedule.

All individuals arrested for a new offence (including those arrested on warrant for an earlier offence) were included in the research. Those transferred in from other stations, or brought from the cells for charging or bailing were excluded, as their official processing time had started before the data collection period. However, for completion, the observational field notes did include details about arrestees not included in the sample in terms of their behaviour on release from custody.

The data collection schedule

The schedule collected both objective and subjective data. Demographic details were collected about each individual arrestee (age, gender, ethnicity, occupation). In addition details of the offence (day, time and location of arrest, and offence type), the custody process (length of time to process, indictors of fitness and well-being), custody decisions taken (detention/release, the need to see a doctor/call a solicitor, warning signs for self-harm or illness), and the time of release were recorded.

Researchers also recorded if arrestees had consumed alcohol and if they were intoxicated as a result. This was ascertained via information that came to light during the custody process (e.g. officers asking arrestees where and how much they had drunk on that night) as well as a subjective assessment on the part of the researchers based on the arrestee's behaviour and any physical or visible signs of intoxication. The researcher recorded on each schedule why they thought the individual was intoxicated by ticking the following series of indicators as appropriate:

- arrestee was seen/admitted consuming alcohol

- arrestee was unsteady on their feet or staggered

- arrestee appeared sleepy

- arrestee smelt of alcohol

- arrestee slurred his/her speech.

While this judgement is undoubtedly a subjective one, the field notes (see below) collected by the second researcher also contained information about observed signs of intoxication. These were useful in checking why decisions were made.

The final section of the schedule contained a two-part qualitative assessment of the behaviour of the arrestee. Behaviours were assessed both in terms of compliance with the custody process and the level of aggression displayed. The level of compliance with the custody process was recorded on a five-point scale (see Box A). The most appropriate description of the level of their compliance was attributed to each arrestee.

Box A: Scale of compliance with the custody process

- **Non-compliant:** does not co-operate with process or procedure. Includes total silence from the arrestee as well as aggressive refusal to answer questions or comply with procedure.
- **Minimally compliant:** Arrestee is almost totally non-compliant, although does co-operate in an extremely limited way – e.g. willingness to provide a name, but nothing else.
- **Semi-compliant:** Arrestee complies with some processes, but not others.
- **Largely compliant:** Arrestee is not totally compliant, but largely co-operates with most procedures – e.g. answers almost all questions, but refuses an answer on one or two things.
- **Fully compliant:** Complies with all processes. However, where an arrestee complies fully but in an aggressive or hostile manner this should be recorded as "fully compliant (hostile)".

To assess displays of physical and verbal aggression in the custody suite, another five-point scale (see Box B) was utilised (based on that outlined in Graham et al., 1997). Unlike the first scale where one overall judgement was made, the aggression scale allowed for any changes and progression in behaviour to be recorded while the arrestee was in custody. For instance, it was possible to distinguish those arrestees who initially used provocative behaviour and language before resorting to medium physical force, from those who maintained the same level of aggression throughout the whole process. Appendix A contains a copy of the data collection schedule.

Box B: Scale of verbal and physical aggression

One-sided provocative behaviour
Offensive, annoying, threatening, provocative behaviour. Might include goading, displays of dominance, general offensive language. This category involves general behaviour, not targeted at anyone specifically.

Verbal arguments/disputes and threats
Any expression of anger or conflict between two or more people, as well as verbal hostility and/or threats. This category relates to abuse/threats being directed at a specific person(s).

Mild physical force or aggression
Incidents in which some physical contact was made as part of verbal aggression, but where the physical contact was aggressive by itself.

Medium physical force or aggression
Includes physical aggression involving pushing, shoving, grabbing, restraining and slapping.

Severe physical aggression and brawls
Involves punching, kicking, head-butting, wrestling, use of a weapon, or many people involved in a physical altercation.

Field notes
Observational field notes were taken in the custody suite throughout each shift. The purpose of these notes was twofold: to provide a level of validation for the data collected via the schedule and to allow the behaviour of arrestees, and the problems associated with them, to be described in more detail. These notes provide a chronological account of each shift observed and give a general overview of the work and atmosphere of the custody suite. Details recorded included the number of arrestees waiting to be processed; where they were located in the custody suite; their physical condition; any displays of aggression or non-compliance; the outcome of searches; arrestees' behaviour in camera cells; and relationships between police officers and arrestees. These notes form the basis for the case studies and examples presented throughout this report.

Semi-structured interviews
In addition to the observational data collection, 31 semi-structured interviews were conducted with operational commanders, beat officers, custody sergeants, police and civilian jailers, licensing officers and local licensees. A custody diversion scheme operated in one site and a worker from the scheme was interviewed, though this is not discussed in this report. Table 1 indicates the number of respondents interviewed by site.

Table 1: Interviewees by site	Site 1	Site 2
Divisional commander	1	1
Custody sergeants	4	2
Police jailer	0	2
Civilian jailer	3	0
Beat officer	4	4
Licensing unit staff	3	3
Licensee	2	1
Custody diversion worker	0	1
Total	17	14

2 See 'The Role of the Forensic Medical Examiner with "Drunken 'Detainees" in Police Custody', Police Research Series Paper 146.

3 Complete interview schedules for each category of professional are available on request.

These interviews covered the range of people that often come into contact with drunken arrestees (except the Forensic Medical Examiner[2]), or who make decisions on policy and practice in this area. The interviews covered a variety of core themes, but were tailored according to the role of the interviewee. The questions mainly covered the following topics:[3]

- a description of the entertainment area on busy Friday or Saturday nights

- the decision-making process when making an arrest

- risk/conflict management, both by the police and licensees

- problems in dealing with drunken arrestees during processing into custody

- suggestions for reducing drunkenness in the city-centre generally

- suggestions for improving the policing of the city-centre late at night

- suggestions for improving the working of the custody suite

- training issues for police.

The interviews were transcribed and systematically coded to draw out themes which emerged throughout the interviews and subsequent analysis (see Sections 5 and 6).

The research sites

Site 1

This city-centre is in the midst of urban regeneration, along a canal system where new luxury flats and town houses are under development. Consequently the entertainment area is becoming busier and more vibrant. At the time of the research there were over 600 licensed premises in the city in pockets dotted around the centre. The main entertainment area is a long street on the edge of the new development and is densely populated with bars, restaurants and clubs.

The police station is situated a short distance away from the main entertainment area. The site custody suite is staffed by two sergeants and up to four civilian jailers. The suite consists of two separate rooms which are used for processing arrestees. One of the rooms is small with one computer terminal which can process only one arrestee at a time. The second larger room is set up to process up to three arrestees at any one time. Arrestees are held until processed in a large holding cell visible from the larger custody processing room. There are 56 holding cells in the station over two floors. These cells are used for both 'live' arrestees (i.e. arrests made by officers on duty) and 'dead' arrestees (i.e. arrestees being held in custody to be taken to court the next day). While the station has the potential to hold 56 arrestees it rarely fills up. Three of the cells were 'camera cells' which allowed the prisoners in them to be watched from the custody suite. These were used primarily for vulnerable prisoners who custody staff judged might injure themselves.

Site 2

The second site is a metropolitan city with a compact city-centre measuring one square mile with over 140 full on-licences and 120 licensed restaurants. Local practitioners report over 75,000 people visiting on a typical Friday night. The city-centre has two distinct entertainment areas existing close to each other but catering for different groups of clientele. The largest of the entertainment areas typically caters for the younger age group. The area's pubs and clubs tend to have loud music, little or no seating and at particular times in the week many run discounted drink nights. The second entertainment area caters for an older and more affluent group. This area has recently been the focus of development and many of the new licensed premises have had a great deal of investment in terms of décor and physical comfort. Alcohol is generally more expensive in the second area.

The police station is situated in the main entertainment area. The site custody suite is staffed by one sergeant and one police jailer. The suite is small and can only process one arrestee at a time. There are two rooms off the custody desk to hold arrestees – one large holding cell and one side room. Arrestees waiting to be processed are held in the holding cell which has bars so any activity is visible. The side room is used mainly to search arrestees and has a door which is closed when searching females. This room is also used for the spill over when a large group are brought in to be processed at the same time or to keep fighting arrestees apart. There are 15 cells in this station all situated at the bottom of a spiral staircase from the processing area. Both 'live' and 'dead' arrestees are held here. There are no camera cells, which means that all checks on arrestees are made by the jailer in person. On busy nights the cells often filled up and the custody staff would be unable to deal with any more arrests until a release was made later in the night. This meant arrestees were taken to another station in the area with officers off the street for longer periods of time as a result.

Structure of the report

Section 2 describes the arrests made during the study. Intoxicated arrestees are compared to those arrestees the researchers believed not to be intoxicated. Section 3 examines the custody process and Section 4 describes the aggression and lack of compliance that can sometimes form a part of the arrestee's behaviour. Sections 5 and 6 provide an account of the views of the police and local licensees of the problem and potential solutions. Finally, Section 7 discusses the main implications for policy and practice.

2. Nature and types of arrests made

This section describes the types of arrestees processed through the two custody suites during the fieldwork period. First, it reports on the number of arrestees processed, their demographic characteristics and the types of offences for which they were arrested. The section then looks at the proportion of arrestees considered to have consumed alcohol and who were intoxicated as a result, and compares the characteristics of intoxicated detainees with those who were not intoxicated.

Number and time of arrest

During the research period 169 arrestees were observed being processed into custody (a mean of six arrestees per study period – 10:30pm to 3.30am).[1] The data, in keeping with previous studies (Hope, 1985; Hobbs et al., 2000), indicates a peak in arrests for the half-hour after pub closing times. More than half of the arrests in this study took place before midnight (88, 52%), peaking at 10.45pm and again at 11.45pm. Numbers arrested varied from night to night with most arrests (107, 63%) made on a Friday, Saturday or Sunday night.[2] There were, however, exceptions to this. Tuesday mornings in Site 2 had as many arrests as a weekend shift, perhaps as a result of cheap drinking promotions being run on a Monday evening to attract custom to the entertainment area.

Reason for and location of arrest

Over a third of the arrestees observed (n=61) were arrested for alcohol-specific offences such as being drunk and disorderly (n=55), drink-driving (n=5) or being in charge of a vehicle while drunk (n=1) (see Table 2). A further quarter were arrested for public order offences (15%) or alleged assault (12%). Overall, 60 per cent of the arrests at the two sites involved disorderly behaviour of some sort.[3] Almost a fifth (16%) of arrestees were arrested for drug-related offences and a tenth for an alleged acquisitive crime such as theft, robbery or burglary.

1 *77 arrestees were observed in Site 1 and 92 in Site 2. This report does not compare the results across the sites because of the relatively small numbers involved, though Table 2 does show the offence distribution in both sites.*

2 *This covers all arrests from 10.30pm on a Friday to midnight on the Sunday.*

3 *Comprising drunk and disorderly, public order offences and assault.*

Table 2: Reason for arrest by site			
N (%)	Site 1	Site 2	Total
Alcohol-specific	12 (15)	49 (53)	61 (36)
Public order	16 (21)	10 (11)	26 (15)
Assault	11 (14)	9 (10)	20 (12)
Drugs	15 (20)	11 (12)	26 (16)
Acquisitive crime	12 (15)	5 (6)	17 (10)
Legal[1]	4 (5)	3 (3)	7 (4)
Criminal damage	2 (3)	1 (1)	3 (2)
Other	5 (7)	4 (4)	9 (5)
Total	77 (100)	92 (100)	169 (100)

1 Wanted on a warrant or breach of bail.

Most arrests were made in the entertainment areas of both centres – either in licensed premises such as pubs or clubs (29%), on the street (56%) or in a fast-food outlet (2%). Alcohol-specific offences, such as being drunk and disorderly, were predominately made in the streets of the entertainment areas (70%), as were assaults (50%) and public order offences (57%). Drug arrests, however, tended to occur on licensed premises (81%).

Characteristics of arrestees

Official statistics published annually by the Home Office and previous research studies (for example, Phillips and Brown, 1998) report that offenders are predominately male. The peak age of offending is 18 for males and 15 for females.[4] In this study, the majority of those arrested were male (141, 83%). The mean age of arrestees observed was 24.6 years and ranged from a juvenile of 12 years to an adult of 53 years. Almost a half of arrestees, among both males and females, were between 18 and 24 years of age.

4 From Criminal Statistics 1999 for cautions and convictions.

Table 3:	Gender and age of arrestees						
N (%)	Under 18	18–24	25–29	30–34	35–39	40 and over	Total
Male	15 (11)	65 (46)	31 (21)	19 (14)	5 (4)	6 (4)	141 (100)
Female	3 (11)	13 (48)	4 (15)	5 (19)	3 (7)	0 (0)	28 (100)

Just over a half of all arrestees observed were unemployed (86, 52%); 42 per cent (70) were employed and seven per cent (11) studying. The proportion unemployed may be an over-estimate as there was evidence on several occasions that individuals were attempting to conceal their occupation for fear of possible repercussions. Most arrestees in the sample were white (149, 88%) with just over ten per cent (18) of black or Asian origin.

While both men and women were equally likely to be arrested for alcohol-specific offences, female arrestees were more likely to be arrested for public order offences (10 females, 36%; 16 males, 11%). Males were more likely to be arrested for assault (18 males, 13%; 2 females, 7%), drug offences (24 males, 17%; 2 females, 7%) and acquisitive offences (16 males, 11%; 1 female, 4%). Arrestees for acquisitive offences were on average younger (20.7 years) than those arrested for public order (23.5 years), alcohol-specific offences (24.6 years), drug-related offences (25.3 years) or assault (25.8 years).

While 26 individuals were arrested for drug offences, a further ten had drugs found in their possession during the routine search in custody – most commonly cannabis or ecstasy. Four arrestees were revealed as previous drug users by Police National Computer checks (3 had been arrested for drug offences). One arrestee requested methadone and eight claimed to be drug users (four of whom were arrested for drug offences). Nothing indicative of drug use other than a drug itself was found in the property of the arrestees.

Alcohol consumption and intoxication among arrestees

The fact that a third of the cohort were arrested for being drunk and disorderly (55, 33%) implies that a significant proportion of the arrestees observed were intoxicated. This study aimed to examine whether those arrested for other offences were also intoxicated with alcohol.

Whether or not the arrestee had consumed any alcohol was ascertained via information that came to light during the custody process (e.g. officers asking arrestees where and how much they had drunk that night) as well as a subjective assessment on the part of the researcher based on the arrestee's behaviour and any physical or visible signs (see Section 1 for fuller discussion). Three-quarters (129, 76%) of arrestees said they had consumed alcohol when asked by custody sergeants. Researchers identified a similar proportion (134, 79%) who had consumed alcohol based on their subjective assessment. Of these 134, three-quarters (100) were considered to be intoxicated; 59 per cent of the total 169 arrestees observed. In five cases the researchers were unable to assess whether or not the arrestee was intoxicated – these cases have been excluded from the analysis.

More than one indicator of intoxication could be recorded about any individual arrestee. The smell of alcohol was the most predominant sign of consumption, being smelt on 116 (69%) of all arrestees observed. This is significant because any individual researcher would be at least two to three yards away during the observation. More than a quarter of arrestees (44, 26%) were staggering, 71 (42%) were slurring their speech and 51 (30%) were visibly sleepy. Perhaps the best way to illustrate how these signs were observed is to describe one case from the field notes. It should be noted that the field notes are a second researcher's view of the events:

> **3.04am (Friday morning)** *Two young males (both 22 years old, one a student and one unemployed) brought in by four officers for being drunk and disorderly. Both restrained but not cuffed. Had been carrying a tree in the middle of the road and when asked to remove it to a safe place did so but minutes later the officers found them putting the tree into the middle of the road again and arrested them.*

> **03.05am** *First male processed. Visibly very drunk. Strong smell of alcohol. Accused officers of behaving like 'louts'. Directed most of his verbal abuse at one particular officer. Complied with all of the custody process but in a sarcastic manner – over-exaggerated politeness. When asked his occupation he replied that he was a student but was going to be a multimedia designer and would 'earn lots of money'. Celled at 3.08am.*

> **03.09am** *Second male processed. Visibly very drunk. Very strong smell of alcohol. Seemed sleepy. Slurred voice. Asked if had to stay overnight. Was told he would be kept to sober up. Claimed he was not drunk and asked if he could walk a white line to prove it. Objected to officers removing his glasses as he could not see anything without them. Was told it was usual and done to prevent self harm. Celled at 03.12am protesting but not needing to be restrained.*

The remainder of this report compares arrestees considered to be intoxicated with alcohol to those who were not intoxicated, in terms of their characteristics and behaviours while in custody. The 34 arrestees who had been drinking but not to the level of intoxication are included in the non-intoxicated group. The term drunken is also used to refer to the intoxicated group.

Characteristics of intoxicated arrestees

Although most of the arrestees whom the researchers identified as being intoxicated were male (80, 80%), females were more likely to be drunk than male arrestees. Over 70 per cent of the 28 female arrestees were thought to be drunk, compared with 58 per cent of male arrestees. Intoxicated and non-intoxicated arrestees were similar in terms of age profile (intoxicated arrestees had a mean age of 24.8 years and age range of 16–47 years; non-intoxicated a mean of 24.7 and range of 12–53 years). Almost three-quarters of drunken arrestees were aged between 18 and 29 years of age, with almost half (48%) being in the 18–24 year old age group. Two-thirds (66%) of arrestees aged 18–24 and three-quarters (74%) of arrestees aged 25 to 29 were intoxicated. Almost two-thirds (63%) of unemployed arrestees were thought to be intoxicated in comparison with 50 per cent of the employed group. The majority of drunken detainees were white (95, 95%).

Intoxicated arrestees: when, where and why arrested

Intoxicated arrestees were usually arrested for disorder offences. 59 per cent were arrested for alcohol-specific offences, 20 per cent for public order offences and a further 12 per cent for assault (Table 4). Non-intoxicated offenders were most likely to be arrested for drugs offences or acquisitive crimes. As would be expected the majority of those arrested for alcohol-specific offences (97%) were thought by the researchers to be drunk. The majority of offenders arrested for public order offences (80%) and most of those arrested for assault (60%) also displayed signs of intoxication. Only two of the 25 arrested for drug offences (possession of and intent to supply Class A or B drugs) appeared to be intoxicated with alcohol during the custody observation. Most of those arrested for acquisitive crime or legal reasons were also sober. Intoxicated arrestees were more likely to be arrested after midnight than non-intoxicated arrestees (55% versus 36%) and more likely to be arrested in the street (66% versus 40%).

Table 4 Reason for arrest by arrestee intoxication		
N (%)	Intoxicated arrestees (n=100)	Non-intoxicated arrestees (n=64[2])
Alcohol-specific	59 (59)	2 (3)
Public order	20 (20)	5 (8)
Assault	12 (12)	8 (13)
Drugs	2 (2)	23 (36)
Acquisitive crime	2 (2)	14 (22)
Legal[1]	2 (2)	5 (8)
Criminal damage	2 (2)	1 (1)
Other	1 (1)	6 (9)

1. Wanted on a warrant or breach of bail.
2. Excludes the 5 arrestees for whom intoxication could not be decided.

Summary

Researchers observed on average six arrestees per night processed into each custody suite with most arrestees being brought into custody on weekend nights. The most likely time of arrest was in the half-hour before and after pub closing time. Most arrests were for disorderly conduct and the majority took place in either the street or in licensed or fast-food premises in the entertainment area. Arrestees observed tended to be white males aged 18 to 29. Over half were unemployed. Almost 80 per cent of the sample had been drinking alcohol and 59 per cent were considered to be intoxicated. Female arrestees, those who were unemployed and those aged 18 to 29 were most likely to exhibit signs of drunkenness. Almost all of those arrested for alcohol-specific offences were thought to be intoxicated, as were 80 per cent of those arrested for public order offences and 60 per cent of those arrested for assault. Drunken arrestees tended to be arrested after midnight, on the street.

3.   Processing arrestees into custody and outcome of arrest

Once arrested, individuals are taken to the police station and booked into the custody suite. The process of 'booking in' is standardised across forces. Every arrestee is asked a standard set of questions to elicit information and undergoes the same process to try to lessen the risk of them coming to harm while in police care. During the custody process basic information about the arrestee's identity are collected (name, date of birth, address). In addition, a basic risk assessment is conducted (health and self-harm) and the arrestee is searched during which any potentially dangerous items, which could be used for self-harm (or to harm custody staff), are removed.

Time taken to process arrestees into custody

Arrestees took an average of 14.7 minutes to be processed through custody (excluding any time spent waiting to be processed during busy periods). However, times to process varied considerably with some individual arrestees being celled after only two minutes while others took over an hour. Three arrestees could not be processed because they were too drunk and four were taken straight to the cells because they were violent. On average it took less time to process an intoxicated arrestee – 12 minutes in comparison with nearly 19 minutes for a non-intoxicated arrestee – with intoxicated arrestees being put into cells quickly because of their condition.

Legal and medical help

While in custody an arrestee has access to legal and medical help. Arrestees are notified of their right to see a solicitor in relation to their alleged offence. Should the arrestee require or request medical attention whilst in custody a Forensic Medical Examiner (FME) will be called to attend to them. FMEs, who are General Practitioners registered to work part-time in this role, make judgements about arrestees' fitness to be interviewed and detained in police custody. For an arrestee who is deemed to be unwell because of ill-health or substance misuse, the FME may prescribe frequent checks by custody staff or be referred immediately to hospital.

Legal assistance
Intoxicated arrestees were less likely to take up their right to see a solicitor – 13 per cent did so compared with 25 per cent of the non-intoxicated cohort. One reason for this is that a third of intoxicated arrestees (35%) were too drunk to even be asked if they wished to take up the right to see a solicitor. Another reason is that the intoxicated group were, in general, arrested for less serious public disorder offences than their non-intoxicated counterparts. Of the 13 intoxicated arrestees who saw a solicitor all were arrested for more serious offences.

Medical help

A quarter (42, 25%) of all arrestees observed were seen by an FME while in custody. Fifteen (9%) had specifically requested to see the FME, a further 27 were seen at the request of the custody sergeant. The FME was most usually called to attend because of injury (10) or to assess fitness to be detained (9). Four were seen because they had been sprayed with CS gas, five because of their illicit drug use, three because of specified illnesses, 1 because they claimed to be in pain and one because they claimed to have swallowed something. Only two were seen specifically because they were drunk. A further seven requested to see an FME but gave no specific reason.

Drunken detainees were more likely than non-intoxicated arrestees to need medical assistance. 30 per cent (30) of those intoxicated were attended by an FME compared with 17 per cent (11) of those who were not intoxicated (it was not possible to assess state of intoxication for one arrestee seen by the FME). Overall, 73 per cent of arrestees attended by the FME were thought by the researcher to be intoxicated.

Of the nine arrestees seen to ascertain if they were fit to be detained six were intoxicated. All of those attended by the FME because of an injury or because they had been sprayed with CS gas during or after their arrest were considered to be intoxicated.

Risk assessment of arrestees

In custody, each arrestee is asked routinely a series of questions by the custody sergeant to determine if there are any physical or mental health problems staff need to be aware of while the arrestee is in their care (see Table 5). A minority (25, 15%) of arrestees observed in this study reported having physical or mental health problems. There were no markers on the custody computer system to alert staff to such risks for most arrested previously.

Of the 25 identified as being at risk, 11 were assessed not to be fit and well (usually because of a known illness, such as asthma, but sometimes because of injury), 13 required medication, seven had previously tried to commit suicide and three were considered to have the potential for self-harm (note that any individual could be placed under more than one category). Table 5 shows that, overall, intoxicated arrestees were less likely to present risk factors than those who were not intoxicated (13% versus 17%). This may be because intoxicated arrestees only needed to 'sleep off' the effects of alcohol or because they were unable to communicate their needs due to their intoxicated state. However, of the 25 arrestees who did report at least one risk factor 17 had consumed alcohol, most of whom (13) were thought to be intoxicated.

Table 5: Risk assessment by custody staff[1] by arrestee intoxication		
N (%)	Intoxicated (n=100)	Non-intoxicated (n=69)
Not fit and well	8 (8)	3 (5)
On medication	4 (4)	9 (14)
Previous suicide attempt	5 (5)	2 (3)
Potential for self-harm	1 (1)	2 (3)
Any risk factor2	13 (13)	12 (17)

1. One arrestee could not answer because he appeared to be intoxicated after using solvents; the remainder were thought to be intoxicated with alcohol.
2. Any arrestee could have more than one risk factor.

Although the proportion of 'at risk' arrestees is relatively small, they do present a significant resource problem. Each arrestee who reports, or is noted as having, a medical or mental health problem requires intensive attention during their period in custody. This may be particularly difficult if they are in custody during the busy weekend periods.

Aside from specific physical or mental health problems, the fact that the majority (59%) of arrestees observed during the fieldwork showed signs of intoxication places a considerable additional burden on custody staff. Arrestees who have consumed alcohol or drugs are one of the most likely groups to die in custody. Two arrestees were deemed so intoxicated that the custody staff felt they must see a Forensic Medical Examiner (FME) to assess if they were fit to be detained and the management they would require if they were deemed fit to be held in custody. An FME's usual course of action with a drunken detainee, if they are fit to be detained, is to prescribe frequent checks – sometimes as often as every 15 minutes.

Length of time held in custody

Time held in custody will depend on the fitness of the arrestee to be detained and/or interviewed, the need to gather evidence and the seriousness of the offence. In total 136 of the 169 arrestees were charged or cautioned with an offence and the timings reported below are based on these arrestees.[1]

1 No further action was taken in eight cases. The rest were bailed pending further inquiries or on police bail (17), had a warrant executed for a previous offence (4) or were summonsed for previous offences (2). Two arrestees were held in police custody to establish their identity.

On average, arrestees who were charged or cautioned were held for 9.2 hours in custody. Length of time in custody varied from 20 minutes (where an arrestee admitted the offence, was processed, cautioned and released) to over three days (where someone was held in custody over a weekend in order to attend court on a Monday morning). Drunken detainees were held on average for less time (8.4 hours) than other detainees (10.1 hours). This is partly accounted for by the fact that the majority of intoxicated detainees were arrested for being drunk and disorderly. This usually results in the detainee being celled to sober up and then released after being cautioned. As a caution implies guilt these offenders are rarely interviewed.

Table 6 below shows average time spent in custody by offence type. The results should be treated with caution given the small number of cases involved. However, the results do indicate that being intoxicated can severely increase the length of time held in custody, particularly for the more serious offences, because arrestees cannot be interviewed while drunk. Intoxicated arrestees charged or cautioned with assault were on average held three times longer than their non-intoxicated counterparts, while intoxicated public order arrestees were, on average, held five times longer.

Disposal of arrestees

Of the 136 cases where action was taken, 83 (61%) were charged with an offence and 53 (39%) were cautioned (see Table 7). The intoxicated group was more likely to be cautioned than the non-intoxicated group (41% vs 33%). Crimes of disorder – drunk and disorderly, assault and public order offences – are predominant. The offence of being drunk and disorderly accounted for 83 per cent of all cautions and 53 per cent of all charges made. Assault (2%) together with public order offences (16%) accounted for a further 18 per cent of all of those charged and a similar proportion of all of those cautioned. Three-quarters (75%) of those charged or cautioned with the assault or public order offences displayed signs of intoxication.

Table 6: Average (mean) length of time spent in custody for offenders charged or cautioned by arrestee intoxication

Offence	Intoxication	Mean time held	N
Drunk and disorderly	Intoxicated	5.8 hrs	57
	Not intoxicated	7.7 hrs	2
Drugs	Intoxicated	3.2 hrs	2
	Not intoxicated	14.9 hrs	21
Acquisitive crime	Intoxicated	32.7 hrs	3
	Not intoxicated	10.5 hrs	9
Assault	Intoxicated	16.9 hrs	5
	Not intoxicated	5.6 hrs	2
Public order	Intoxicated	11.4 hrs	16
	Not intoxicated	2.4 hrs	4
Drink driving	Intoxicated	11.3 hrs	4
	Not intoxicated	.33 hrs	1
Total	Intoxicated	8.4 hrs	87
	Not intoxicated	10.1 hrs	39
	Total	9.2 hrs	126[1]

1. Ten of the 136 arrestees were excluded from the analysis: it could not be decided if three arrestees were intoxicated; a further seven spread across five further offence categories were too small in number for analysis.

Table 7: Offence for which arrestee was charged or cautioned by arrestee intoxication

N (%)	Intoxicated	Not intoxicated
Caution	36 (41)	15 (33)
Charge	50 (58)	30 (65)
Juvenile caution	1 (1)	1 (2)
Totals[1]	87 (100)	46 (100)

1. For three of the 136 charged or cautioned, researchers were unsure if the arrestee was intoxicated hence are excluded from the Table.

Summary

Intoxicated arrestees were processed more quickly into custody than non-intoxicated arrestees, often because of the condition they were in. They were more likely to be seen by a Forensic Medical Examiner than the non-intoxicated group. This seems to be because the custody staff were aware of the risk of detaining a drunken individual and often took extra precautions as a result. However, intoxicated arrestees were less likely to see a solicitor, often because they were too drunk to be asked if they wished to take up this right, although those charged with more serious offences did see a solicitor. Custody staff were aware that intoxication was a risk to the well-being of arrestees and there was evidence throughout this research that the 100 arrestees who were drunk placed an additional time burden on the custody staff. While on average intoxicated arrestees were held in custody for less time than the non-intoxicated group, intoxication severely increased the length of time arrestees were held in custody for some offences. This was particularly the case for more serious offences because they could not be interviewed while drunk. Intoxicated arrestees were more likely to be cautioned than those who were not intoxicated.

4. Arrestees' levels of compliance and aggression

In order to describe the nature of the problems arrestees – particularly drunken arrestees – cause in custody, several measures of the behaviour of arrestees were recorded. This section discusses arrestees' levels of compliance with the custody process and the levels of verbal or physical aggression displayed. It also explores some of the other additional problems created by detainees while in custody. Short case studies are used to describe in more depth the problems individual detainees can cause.

Compliance with the custody process

Researchers rated individual arrestees' compliance with the custody process along a five-point scale from compliance through to non-compliance (see Section 1 for discussion). This scale is used in conjunction with examples from the field notes to demonstrate not just the severe disruption that arrestees can cause the police but also the way in which the custody process can be slowed by a lack of co-operation.

Nearly two-thirds (108) of arrestees were described by the researchers as compliant during the custody process. However, intoxicated arrestees were more likely to be non-compliant than those who were not intoxicated. Around a half (49%) of intoxicated arrestees displayed some level of non-compliance (including complying but in a hostile manner), compared with a tenth (11%) of those who were not intoxicated (see Table 8). Among intoxicated arrestees 12 per cent were completely non-compliant, a further ten per cent were only minimally or semi-compliant, nine per cent were largely compliant and 16 per cent were compliant but in a hostile manner. Two arrestees were too drunk to be processed and were carried straight through the custody suite to a cell.

Among all those assessed to be non-compliant (both intoxicated and non-intoxicated), most were arrested for alcohol-specific offences (33), public order offences (9) or assault (5). Their non-compliance may well have been an extension of the behaviour for which they had been arrested. The brief descriptions below illustrate the various levels of non-compliance observed and the types of behaviour custody officers have to cope with.

N (%)	Intoxicated arrestees	Non-intoxicated arrestees
Table 8 Compliance with custody process by arrestee intoxication		
Non-compliant	12 (12)	0
Minimally compliant	2 (2)	0
Semi-compliant	8 (8)	2 (3)
Largely compliant	9 (9)	1 (2)
Fully compliant (hostile)	16 (16)	4 (6)
Fully compliant	51 (51)	57 (89)
Too drunk to be processed	2 (2)	0
Total[1]	100 (100)	64 (100)

1. The researchers were unable to say whether or not five of the 169 observed individuals were intoxicated.

Totally non-compliant

A small number (12) of arrestees were totally non-compliant with the custody process, co-operating with no process or procedure. This varied from total silence to aggressive refusal to answer questions or comply with procedures. These arrestees caused a great deal of disruption and extra work. All were thought to have consumed alcohol and were visibly intoxicated as a result. Nine were arrested on the street and all displayed a level of aggression in the custody suite, varying from being verbally abusive to being seriously physically aggressive. Eight were brought in hand-cuffed and most needed to be restrained during their processing. For example:

11.25pm (Friday night) *27 year old male arrested at a restaurant after urinating in the hallway after being refused service because he is very drunk. Did not seem to be able to stand without leaning on the counter. Head hung down as if he could not hold it up. Refused to co-operate – would not give name or address. Speech was very slurred – only words that could be clearly heard are obscenities. Needed to be restrained to be searched but not really able to put up a fight although he tried. Two officers were needed to put him in a cell – while he kept saying 'get off us' over and over again.*

Minimal compliance

Two arrestees, both intoxicated, were minimally compliant. They co-operated in an extremely limited way, perhaps only providing their name, but no other information. For example:

11.52pm (Friday night) *22 year old male arrested under Section 4 of the Road Traffic Act and on suspicion of theft. Researcher smells alcohol. He appeared annoyed and agitated. Although he was polite at the beginning of the process he became increasingly sarcastic. It emerged that he had given a false name to the officers. He removed his property without being asked to and during the routine search he dropped a wrap on to the floor which he claims was 'weed'. He was then arrested for possession of an illegal substance. He was not happy with the officer needing to go through his pockets stating the was 'not a criminal, not a thief'. He complained of being unwell – 'my gut is hurting, and it feels like I might have a fit'. He tried to answer his mobile phone and refused to give his necklace to the custody staff becoming aggressive to the point where the staff felt he was too aggressive to process any further.*

Semi-compliant

A further ten (again the majority were intoxicated) were described as being semi-compliant with the custody process: they answered most questions but caused disruption. For example:

11.45 pm (Saturday night) *20 year old male arrested for being drunk and disorderly. He was upset at being told that he would be put in the cells. He refused to take his necklace off but then did so. He was arrested for urinating in the street, but claimed he was just being sick. He refused to answer questions, then got verbally aggressive but was celled without incident.*

Largely compliant

Ten arrestees (9 of whom displayed signs of intoxication) were described as largely compliant with the custody process – answering most of what was asked of them but at some level unco-operative. For example, the following arrestee took 20 minutes to be processed because of his behaviour:

> **01.25am (Saturday)** *28 year old male arrested because wanted on warrant processed into custody. Very visibly drunk. Slurred voice, unsteady on his feet, sleepy looking, didn't seem to comprehend what was being said to him. Researcher smelt alcohol. Arresting officer knew him and answered custody questions for him as prisoner could not. Moved very slowly and deliberately while searching his pockets to find his address.*

> **01.28am** *Arrestee moved away from the desk and had to be directed back by the arresting officer. Asked to see doctor and solicitor because 'I am unlawfully arrested'. When asked how much he had to drink he replied 'I am an alcoholic'. Officers searched (outer clothing) in view of the researchers. Compliant. Kept asking "Can I go?" "Can I go to cells please?" "What was I arrested for?", "Can I have a solicitor?" Laughs.*

> **01.45am** *Arrestee asked for a doctor again – 'I am suffering from the DTs'. Celled to sober up.*

Compliant but hostile

Twenty arrestees (16 of whom displayed signs of intoxication) were described as compliant but hostile, co-operating but being sarcastic or rude. For example:

> **00.00am (Tuesday morning)** *28 year old male was compliant but very stressed – the arresting officers advised him to 'chill out' – he said he could not because he felt so stupid – he complained about drug policy and laws. While compliant he continued to be mildly sarcastic throughout processing. He complained about being searched.*

Levels of aggression

Aggressive behaviour was measured in two ways. First, the researchers recorded whether or not the arrestee was handcuffed on arrival at the custody suite – an indication that restraint was required to make the arrest – and if further restraint was used while they were in custody. Second, the researchers recorded levels of aggression displayed throughout the custody process using a five-point scale (see Section 1).

The use of restraint

Nearly 40 per cent (66) of arrestees were in handcuffs on entering the custody suite. A third of those brought in handcuffed (22) had been arrested for being drunk and disorderly, and a further quarter (17) for an alleged public order offence. Just under a fifth (12) were arrested for drug offences and just over a tenth (8) for assault. The vast majority (80%) of those brought in handcuffed showed signs that they had consumed alcohol and 64 per cent were intoxicated. The intoxicated group were more likely to be hand-cuffed on arrival (42%) than the non-intoxicated group (35%).

Generally, individuals tended to calm down enough to have the hand-cuffs removed once the custody process began. However, there were incidents in both sites when arrestees were taken straight to the cells because of the level of aggression they were displaying. The need to restrain an arrestee once in the custody suite was not frequent but not unusual. In total 29 arrestees had to be restrained while in the custody suite, 20 of whom had arrived hand-cuffed. Often the issue which caused arrestees to become agitated was the routine removal of property, particularly personal items such as jewellery.

> *00.43am (Friday morning)* 28 year old male arrested for assault with a bottle in a night club. He was brought into the custody suite handcuffed and accompanied by five officers. Visibly drunk, slurred words. Clothing was blood stained and he had cuts on his face. Claimed to have cut his ear by banging it on the van when arrested – stressed that it was his own fault. Asked to see doctor for cut. "I've never been arrested for fighting before". Compliant but became agitated at times – when asked to remove his wedding ring he got very upset and refused to hand it over. It took 3 officers to restrain him to remove his ring, resulting in a scuffle which ended up in a side room. The ring was removed and he appeared to calm down. He asked several times why he had to have his property removed. Custody sergeant explained that they are responsible for the safe keeping of his property.

On several occasions the individual was too intoxicated to be reasoned with. For example, one young woman was brought into custody after being found wandering in the middle of a busy road. She looked very young – but was in her late teens – and caused a great deal of work for the custody staff during the time she was detained:

01.00am (Tuesday morning) *17 year old female brought in restrained by two officers. Reported for her safety by a member of the public who thought she was a young child. She kicked custody desk and officers constantly while screaming, shouting and using obscene language. A female officer was called to search her. She urinated on the floor. She is constantly verbally abusive. The female officer asked where she stands on health and safety as the female arrestee was saturated with urine. Four officers were needed to restrain her during the search – this took nearly ten minutes and she was immediately celled as she was too drunk to process in the normal way – she continued to kick and scream and had to be restrained to get her into a cell.*

01.13am *Second female officer arrives to help restrain the young female. Male officer advises the female officer that she "…will need glove".*

01.22am *FME visited female arrestee. She needed to be restrained by two female officers during examination and was put in camera cell to be observed.*

01.27am *FME back in custody suite. Stated he is in no position to assess female arrestee as he could not examine her properly. Screaming on-going. Advises that she be re-assessed in the morning.*

01.56am *Female arrestee still screaming.*

02.10 am *Cleaner arrives to clean up urine.*

02.30am *Female arrestee no longer screaming – but still shouting.*

02.05pm (Tuesday afternoon) *Charged with being drunk and disorderly and released.*

Displays of aggression

Like the scale of compliance the aggression scale helped to demonstrate how the behaviour of individual arrestees could affect the custody environment both by slowing down the process itself and by placing those working in the suite at risk. Displays of aggression were recorded on a scale ranging from one-sided provocative behaviour to severe physical aggression. Escalation of aggression was recorded as the arrestee was processed and therefore for any individual arrestee more than one recording of aggression level could be made.

Almost 30 per cent of arrestees displayed aggression of some sort during the custody process. Those in the intoxicated group were significantly more likely to be aggressive (42% in comparison with only 8% of the non-intoxicated group). For almost a third of the aggressive arrestees (16) the level of aggression escalated during the custody process and most of these again were intoxicated (13). Again this seems a small number but these arrestees have a great deal of potential to cause problems, including injury to themselves and others.

Table 9 illustrates the levels of aggression observed in the custody suite by whether or not the arrestee was intoxicated. The Table includes multiple entries for arrestees who displayed different levels of aggression while in custody. Where aggression was displayed it tended to be in the form of verbal abuse with displays of severe physical aggression rare. Brief descriptions of aggressive individuals and their behaviour are given below to illustrate the types of behaviour custody staff face.

Table 9 Levels of aggression in the custody suite by arrestee intoxication		
N (%)	Intoxicated arrestees (n=100[1])	Non-intoxicated arrestees (n=64[1])
No aggressive behaviour	58 (58)	59 (92)
One-sided provocative	27 (27)	2 (3)
Verbal arguments	17 (17)	3 (5)
Mild physical force	7 (7)	3 (5)
Medium physical force	1 (1)	0 (0)
Severe physical force	6 (6)	0 (0)

1. Aggressive arrestees who displayed different levels of aggression while in custody have been counted under each level of aggression displayed.
2. The researchers could not say whether five arrestees were intoxicated or not.

One-sided provocative aggression
Most of the arrestees who displayed one-sided provocative aggression did so by being provocative, annoying or threatening but not directing it at a specific individual:

01.55am (Saturday morning) 28 year old male arrested for being drunk and disorderly brought into holding cell handcuffed. Talked continuously. Slurred voice. Researcher notes he smelt strongly of alcohol. His shirt was unbuttoned and blood on it. Complained loudly that he had paid for a hotel. He claimed he was being unfairly treated. Police officer stated he had resisted arrest. Arrestee remains unco-operative throughout processing. Very sarcastic to arresting officer 'try please and thank you'. He asked to look at the computer and generally was disruptive. He then defecated in his trousers and claimed that it happened when he was kicked to the floor 'without consent'. The staff were unable to process him fully as he requested to be taken to his cell to clean himself up.

Verbally argumentative

Twenty arrestees were verbally argumentative, attempting to argue with custody staff or arresting officers. The intoxicated group was more likely to display this type of behaviour (17% vs 5% of the non-intoxicated group). This, again, may severely slow down the booking in of the individual.

00.01am (Saturday morning) 18 year old male was shouting in holding cell. "Cannot believe this! I get kicked all over the street and get arrested for it. I am not saying a thing until I get released" Very confrontational – used a great deal of bad language directed at the arresting officer. Repeatedly asked if he could get a taxi home and was told when he had sobered up. Suddenly started to cry "I am sorry". Sat down on bench and put his hands between the slats of the bench and leant forward crying. "Please let me get a taxi home – I am sorry". Tried to appeal directly to the sergeant "Can I get a taxi home sarge? I am sorry, just me being a bit loud on the drink".

Physical force

Where physical force was used it was mostly of a mild nature with the main part of the aggression being verbal. In a small number of cases (6) the force used by the arrestee was at a severe level involving punching, kicking, head-butting or wrestling. All six displayed signs of intoxication.

02.18am (Friday morning) 19 year old female brought to the custody suite desk for processing. She is shouting, screaming and kicking out. She is handcuffed. A scuffle breaks out and she is taken by police officers to a holding cell. She continues to shout and scream.

02.46am Taken straight through custody suite, still handcuffed, by two officers to cell kicking and screaming. She sets off the cell alarm and one female in the holding cell says 'they're killing people in the cells – do you hear that'.

Other issues

While aggression and non-compliance with the custody process causes problems for the police, there were a number of other issues which became evident during the course of the fieldwork. These are discussed below.

Hygiene

Hygiene, particularly when dealing with drunken detainees can be a significant problem. Several arrestees defecated or urinated in their clothing during or after arrest. These arrestees were then supplied with a white paper garment to change into, with their clothes being placed in a plastic bag. At best this can be unpleasant for the officers involved when the arrestee is compliant and agrees to change their clothing. At worst it can be a health and safety issue if an arrestee refuses to change clothing. As described earlier, in one case a female officer searched a female arrestee who was soaked in urine. Some officers did express worry about the potential to contract infectious diseases, particularly hepatitis C.

Female arrestees

Female arrestees can present particular problems in a busy custody suite. Both sites required that a female officer searched female prisoners and was present if necessary during procedures such as a consultation with an FME. In itself this should not be a problem, however, neither site had a female officer as part of the custody team during the research period (although in Site 1 there was often a female civilian jailer on duty[1]) and consequently female officers often had to be called into the custody suite to deal with female arrestees. This resulted in female officers being taken away from their normal duties and as discussed in Section 5 also led to some resentment among the officers. Female arrestees were equally as capable as males of being obstructive.

1 *Civilian Detention Officers (unlike police officers) have no right to search an arrestee who refuses to be searched.*

11.12pm (Friday night) *Two laughing females staggered into custody suite (26 and 24 years of age) accompanied by two police officers. They were shouting and arguing continuously – "I cannot believe this is happening". "You are a fucking bastard" – to male officer.*

11.20pm (Friday night) *First female brought to counter to be processed. Verbally aggressive. "Am I going to be here all night? You think you can lock someone up for nothing. You want to lift the right fucking people." "I have never been arrested in my life." Using a lot of bad language but compliant with process. Buzzer sounding from cells – "aren't you supposed to do something about that".*

Noise and general disruption

Another significant issue is noise. On many occasions an arrestee could bang repeatedly on the door of their cell, or shout for hours on end. For example, one female arrestee arrested early in the night created a disturbance for the whole of the research period until 3.30am.

> **10.30pm (Tuesday night)** *Two women (one in her 40s and one in her early 20s) arrested for being drunk and disorderly. The older of the two women had already been processed and was in the side room. She appeared to have been very aggressive and two police women were needed to search her. As she was at risk, she was 'white suited' i.e., her own clothes were removed and she was dressed in a disposable white overall. Through the whole process she shouted and argued and protested her innocence. Two female officers were needed to take her to the cells. She could be heard shouting and banging on the cell door until 10.52pm.*

> **10.59pm.** *Banging and shouting started again from female cells. Female needed to see FME. FME refused to see her without two officers present.*

> **11.09pm** *Woman brought from cells to see FME. Crying 'I've done nothing wrong...'*

> **11.26pm** *Woman came back into custody suite after seeing FME accompanied by female officer. Laughed and joked but began to shout again on the way back to the cell.*

> **11.34pm** *Woman screaming and banging in cells.*

> **11.35pm** *FME returned to talk to custody sergeant. He wanted the woman held for a minimum of six hours to sober up plus regular checks. FME commented that he thought she might be epileptic but it was difficult to be accurate as she was too drunk to give her medical history.*

> **11.42pm.** *Banging in cells began again. This banging on cell door and shouting continued intermittently until end of the study period at 3.30am.*

Assessing risk

A significant responsibility, particularly for the custody sergeant who must make judgements on fitness to be detained and interviewed, is to judge the necessity of calling out a Forensic Medical Examiner or sending an individual to the local Accident and Emergency department. Sometimes an arrestee who is intoxicated may at first appear worse than they actually are. For example:

10.45pm (Tuesday night) *21 year old female was sleeping in the holding cell. An officer attempted to rouse her by speaking to her but got no response. He shook her shoulder to wake her. It took approximately one minute to get her to her feet. She was visibly very drunk. Two officers had to assist her to her feet and to support her while she walked to the counter. She appeared to have difficulty standing and put her head on the counter. The custody sergeant had to speak to her several times to get her to stand up by herself. She then seemed okay and took part in the custody process without any further incident.*

Potential for group violence

Where a group of individuals are arrested in the same incident a fight can continue in the custody suite. The researchers witnessed problems with single sex groups of young men and women where the situation remained volatile until they were separated and celled. One particular incident involved a group of young women in Site 1. This group caused problems not only because they verbally abused each other but also because their behaviour was at times violent and generally unpredictable. All demonstrated signs of intoxication:

02.15am *Following a report of a fight outside a pub 2 females arrived in the custody suite.*

02.18am *21 year old female brought to the desk handcuffed and shouting/screaming. She scuffled with the officers and was put into holding cell to calm down. She continued shouting and screaming. Second female (23 years old) brought into the holding cell and shouted at the first girl. Third female (21 years) arrived in holding cell. All shouting at each other while first female cried about the handcuffs*

02.46am *First female kept shouting and screaming and began to kick and scream when an officer attempted to process her and as a result was taken straight to cell by two officers while she continued to kick and scream. An alarm was set off. The second female in the holding cell shouts 'they're killing people in the cells – do you hear that'.*

02.47am *Third female carried through custody to cells while shouting and kicking. The second Female began to argue with arresting officer – saying that it is all lies – said she's pregnant and she's had five miscarriages already – claimed that the officers pushed and squeezed her. She complained that the Custody Sergeant is rude while at the same time was herself very rude to WPC.*

03.30am *Second female brought to desk. She became flirtatious with arresting officer. She then refused to move, and sat on the floor, and needed to be restrained and carried through to cell by six officers. Screaming and shouting continued from the cells.*

Summary

This research observed a small number of arrestees who were non-compliant or aggressive or both. These individuals have a great deal of potential to cause extra work for a busy custody suite. The intoxicated group were more likely to be non-compliant and aggressive than the non-intoxicated group. About a half (49%) of intoxicated arrestees were non-compliant to some degree and 42 per cent were aggressive. A number of other problems were identified during the research which were particularly associated with intoxicated arrestees including health and safety, problems associated with processing/caring for female arrestees, noise levels, responsibility of judging whether an arrestee was fit to be detained and the potential for violence.

5. Perceptions of policing the late night city-centre

This section discusses the views and perceptions of police officers, licensees and civilian custody staff regarding the problems which arose in the two city-centres due to drunkenness, the factors which influenced whether or not officers decided to arrest drunken offenders, and officers' views on the problems created by drunken arrestees in the custody suite.

Police and licensees' perceptions of the late night city-centres

Both the police and licensees perceived individuals who were drunk as a problem within both city-centres studied. For licensees the issue was one of needing to ensure there were adequately trained staff to eject or refuse entry to individuals or to refuse service of more alcohol to intoxicated individuals. The police were concerned with public disorder on the streets and ensuring the safety of the public and individuals arrested. Alcohol was seen as contributing to nuisance crime in the late night city-centre environment more so than serious violent crime, but most feared the presence of alcohol could escalate a minor disagreement into a more dangerous situation:

> There is an aggression they offer to you and an uncertainty about how they will act...especially if they are in a group of people.(Beat officer, Site 1)

The police distinguished between types of drinkers, describing two main groups that they come into contact with. During the day they dealt with what they often referred to as 'habitual drunks' or 'winos' who tended to drink in public places and were involved with the police on a regular basis for petty crime. If they were involved in disorder or violence it was usually with members of their own drinking group. The second group were the weekend 'binge' drinkers who consumed large amounts of alcohol in single drinking sessions. These were identified as generally young men who in the main, they believed, were not likely to have offended previously:

> Anything from mid teens to mid to late 20s, more often than not white. Generally working. They weren't rough people...they had jobs. Occasionally they had minor convictions but usually nothing. Often they had not had any experience of the police and would decide to answer back or fight back and would get arrested. (Custody sergeant, Site 1)

Both of these groups had potential to cause problems for the police but different types of problems. The 'habitual' group were seen as causing problems which generally affected themselves or the group they drank with. For the custody staff, the 'habitual' drunk was generally seen as less violent and mostly only disturbed the general public by being visible. However, they posed particular problems in terms of their own care while in custody:

> I suppose the alcoholics are usually less violent, they usually come in and the main problem with them is watching for their own safety you know. (Civilian custody officer, Site 2)

However, the younger 'binge' drinking group was seen as having more potential for violence and disorder:

> The young people it's more the violent side, getting them into the cells in the first place, and then they usually cause a row when they're in there. (Police Custody officer, Site 2.

Arresting a drunken offender

While the study did not observe officers making arrests, the interviews did explore the process by which they make decisions to arrest an individual who is drunk. The overwhelming thread that ran through interviews was of officers rationalising the need to arrest. Officers on the street can exercise discretion in any decision to arrest. In the case of someone considered to be drunk it would seem that rarely is an arrest automatic but that officers routinely try to calm a situation down before deciding to arrest or not. Generally, officers appear to have a lenient attitude towards inebriates, although the attitude of the individual was paramount in most encounters:

> It is actually an offence to be drunk in a public place but most people are okay and we don't arrest the whole of (site 2) on a Friday night. So the ones that are being disorderly, for example someone urinating on the pavement, we wouldn't normally arrest for that unless they start giving you grief….they won't give you their name or they start giving you a load of abuse back … I think this is why should we have to put up with that. (Beat officer, Site 2)

The offender's physical condition is also a factor considered. If they are so drunk that they run a risk of injuring themselves or making themselves vulnerable to becoming a victim of crime then an arrest is made for their own protection. The potential for violence or other crime is paramount in any decision. If an officer feels that an individual will commit a further offence or that members of the public are at risk then an arrest is the likely outcome:

But you will always get the one who sees the uniform that have got to have a pop - that have got to have a go and show off to their friends. If that happens and they have ignored that warning then they will be arrested particularly where it is whipping other people up against you and you have the potential for a bigger incident of disorder. As for seeing some one slurring their words [just] walking along not annoying anyone then no. If you do that you are desperate. (Beat officer, Site 1)

Both sites had very busy custody suites, particularly during weekend nights. Officers were aware that the suites often filled up quickly and admitted that it sometimes affected their decision to arrest, especially when an offence is viewed as being minor. While there were other suites available, they were some distance away and would involve a longer time off the streets because of travelling time and the need to return to caution/charge. As officers were aware of the potential for violence they employed various strategies for subduing potential arrestees and the individual's reaction to these strategies ultimately affected the decision to arrest or not. Officers felt that the essential element in dealing with intoxicated individuals on the street was experience. Few officers believed that any training could prepare a person for the reality of dealing with a drunk. All officers described attempting to calm individuals by 'talking them down':

I try and just bring it down by, I mean a lot of them give you verbal challenges, you know if I saw you on your own without your uniform you know bla, bla, bla this that and t'other. I never rise to any of that I just ask them to do what I want them to do, and hopefully if they are shouting and screaming just keep your voice down and don't be confrontational with them. If I ask them to do something, I ask them politely, and then if they don't respond to that I ask them firmly. (Police custody officer, Site 2).

The importance of gaining some sort of rapport with the individual was underlined by several officers. Although officers reported this can be difficult where an intoxicated individual is verbally abusive. Consequently, when verbal attempts to calm an individual down fail, officers sometimes have to apply physical restraint. Physical restraint was only spoken of when other attempts to calm an individual down do not work.

Problems caused by drunken detainees

The police officers identified several key problems caused by drunken arrestees: the potential to be violent or aggressive and the additional time and resource demands involved in processing drunken arrestees and caring for them while being detained.

Violence and aggression

All the officers interviewed had experienced violence, at least at a verbal if not physical level, as a result of a confrontation with a drunken arrestee. Some had been involved in more serious incidents where they were in physical danger.

> *We turned up to an incident in a notorious hotspot for drink related crime just opposite the X nightclub. There is a fish and chip shop there and a couple of kebab places and stuff like that and there was a fight started, there was pushing going on and I was with a more experienced officer. We decided to intervene beforehand rather than radio as quite a nasty fight had begun in front of us. As we tried to arrest the offenders we were just pulled off, mobbed by a lot of friends and passers by. It is a very busy area, hundreds of people around there and the WPC got knocked to the ground and tried to hold on to this guy and got dragged along a bit. (Beat officer, Site 1)*

Verbal abuse directed at beat officers and custody staff was commonplace in this study. Most staff did not react and custody sergeants in both sites used this technique as a matter of course. Often the prisoner would instantly calm down once in front of the custody sergeant. It would seem because the sergeant is a figure of authority, and not directly involved in the incident which led to the arrest, he/she became a focus for the arrestees complaints:

> *People that are verbally hostile – you just don't react. Eventually they weary of it. If you can see somebody is going to kick off in a big way or they become particularly aggressive, just put them straight in the cell. It's pointless talking to somebody who is getting more and more excited, not giving the information you want. (Custody sergeant, Site 2).*

When asked if the constant abuse sometimes affected them, few said that it did. It was seen as part of the job. Many spoke of almost going on auto-pilot when facing potentially dangerous situations:

> *You do worry about safety but when you are confronted adrenalin kicks in and you don't think of your own circumstances then. (Civilian custody officer, Site 1).*

Processing time and care in custody

The police have a duty of care to every person arrested and taken into custody, both in terms of their legal rights and their physical well-being. When individuals are under the influence of alcohol this can put even more demands on a busy custody suite. The main worry for custody staff is the physical well-being of the prisoner because the officer on duty may be held liable if they come to any harm. Officers described drunken arrestees as time-consuming. They were seen as taking longer to process and also to care for once in custody. The custody process often could be incomplete simply because the intoxicated individual was unable or unwilling to give the necessary information:

> *...because they are drunk or under the effects of alcohol, they are not going to be quite as compus mentis as the average person is, therefore the booking in procedure is actually going to take longer, because you are probably going to have to ask some of the questions three or four times before you get a sensible answer. (Licensing inspector, Site 1)*

In both sites drunken arrestees were held for a minimum of four hours to sober up. Often these arrestees took up extra time because of the need to be aware of the potential for them to injure themselves by falling or suffocating on their own vomit. Consequently, arrestees were checked regularly and often roused from their sleep to ensure they were conscious. These checks may be as frequent as every 15 minutes and each check must be recorded on the custody record, so putting some degree of pressure on custody officers.

> *(When the doctor) comes in and says 15 minute checks, can you imagine doing 15 minute check when you have got five or six people in a cage and you have a full custody suite. (Civilian custody officer, Site 1)*

A doctor was called if the arrestee was judged as needing to see one because of his/her intoxication or was injured or unwell. However, calling a doctor sometimes required the presence of another officer if the arrestee was violent or aggressive. Some officers believed that a hospital or a detoxification unit was the best place for arrestees who were particularly drunk.

> *If they are drunk and disorderly then yeah they have to come in really, if they are drunk and incapable then they should go to hospital. Because there's health implications there and they could die. And if you've got a fear they're going to be sick, choking on vomit, the place to be is hospital, not the police station. But if they're violent they have to be. (Custody sergeant, Site 1)*

Custody officers in site 2 worked in very cramped conditions. In particular the fact that the cells were down a flight of spiral stairs caused a great deal of problems, especially when the individual was reluctant. In addition, the design of the custody block had a knock-on effect for the jailer who cared for the arrestees once celled. Again, the difficulties could be magnified if the arrestee required extra attention or was very demanding as prisoners who needed regular checks were physically far away from the custody desk itself where staff were based, and as such the jailer could be out of earshot of the sergeant.

Female detainees

There were more male than female officers on duty in both sites. This reflects the gender balance of the arrestees they deal with. However, the limited number of female custody officers can cause problems when dealing with female arrestees who need female staff to undertake certain duties with or for them. Often a female officer has to be brought in from team duties to do this work. There was some evidence that these officers resented this burden and in particular that it took them away from what they were on duty to do at that particular night. It was not just the female officers who noted this.

> It is an enormous bone of contention with female officers on that unit .... there are two female officers on my shift of eight people, and they were often called to deal with prisoners from other sectors, which has got nothing to do with them personally. They were called in to sit at cells and go and do searches and it just annoys them basically. They are singled out for mundane and unfair treatment. (Beat officer, Site 1)

Most of the male staff interviewed did not like to deal with female arrestees and many spoke of actively attempting not to arrest women because they were perceived as less violent. However, when arrested the overwhelming belief is that female arrestees had the potential to cause as many if not more problems than males – most likely because officers arrest only the worst female offenders. Officers generally felt that they could not be as aggressive with a female arrestee, even if they were being as violent or verbally abusive as male arrestees:

> If you are going to tussle with a bloke, fair enough, if you are having a fight with a female, you actually have to be a bit more careful how you handle them physically where you touch them. Otherwise they are going to start making allegations, rightly or wrongly. (Licensing Inspector, Site 1)

Summary

Police and licensees considered drunks to be a problem within the city-centre, although contributing more to nuisance crime than serious crime. Two groups of problematic drinkers were identified. 'Habitual drunks' were usually a daytime problem disturbing the public by their presence, whereas weekend 'binge' drinkers were seen as having more potential for violence and disorder. Officers consider a number of factors when arresting a drunk including the attitude of the individual, the offender's physical condition; the potential for violence or another crime and the current capacity of the custody suite. Strategies for dealing with drunks included trying to calm the situation by building rapport with the individual, though if this failed physical restraint could be employed. Officers regarded receiving verbal abuse as being part of the job. Intoxicated individuals were seen by officers as time and resource consuming. The occasional lack of female staff to deal with female arrestees placed an additional burden on other female officers on duty to attend a custody suite on request.

6.   Alleviating the problem

This research describes the processing into custody of intoxicated arrestees during the night shift at two city-centre police stations. It provides an insight into the problems faced by police officers and civilian staff in attempting to maintain order in the late night custody suite. The numbers of arrests seem few (9 on an average weekend night per site) given that each of these city-centres entertainment areas cater for thousands of people. However, to put this into context, at both sites there were only on average ten officers (in the custody suite and on the street) on duty during any study period. At least two officers dealt with each prisoner (more if the arrestee had been violent); and between the custody process, preparation of evidential notes and the charging or cautioning of the individual they could be removed from the streets for up to two hours – 25 per cent of any shift. Consequently, the arresting and processing of these offenders significantly reduced the visible presence of officers on the street.

Alcohol had been consumed by the majority of arrestees in this study and most of these were detained for disorderly behaviour. Researchers observed signs of intoxication in nearly two-thirds of the sample. Intoxicated arrestees often needed extra attention because of the condition they were in. In site 2 at any given time there were only two custody staff on duty – with one jailer responsible for all checks on prisoners. As such, these arrestees accounted for a substantial amount of additional work.

The tackling of alcohol-related crime involves examining the issue from the perspective of the entertainment area, the custody suite and the larger community. There is some evidence that a multi-agency approach, including police, local authority, treatment services and the licensed trade, works best in dealing with this issue. Appendix B displays the tools which might be usefully adopted at a local level. Much of this work has been carried out in Australia (for example, Turning Point, 1998; Lang and Rumbold, 1997), but important initiatives have also been undertaken in the UK.[1] Initiatives have included addressing transportation issues, the location of fast food outlets, encouraging licensee codes of practice, training and registration of door staff (Purser, 1997), training of bar staff, Pub-watch and Pub-ban schemes (MCM Research, 1993; Portman Group, 1998), as well as intelligence-led strategies.

The remainder of this report will discuss the situational, prevention and enforcement initiatives which might be considered in any long term strategy to reduce crime in the late night city-centre and potential strategies to alleviate the problems in the custody suite. The latter receives most attention given that the custody suite was the main focus of this study. For a fuller discussion of the issues around reducing crime in the late night city centre see Deehan (1999), Hobbs et al. (2000) or Hope (1985).

1   *In particular, the Home Office Crime Reduction Programme is currently undertaking evaluations of several local city-centre initiatives under the auspices of the Targeted Policing Initiative.*

Reducing alcohol-related crime in the city-centre entertainment area

Situational prevention

Situational prevention refers to measures taken by the police or other agencies to reduce the opportunities for crime to be committed in specific places (Jacobson, 1999). There were several levels at which situational crime prevention operated in the two sites both as a deterrent and as a means of extending formal surveillance. The main measures were the use of technology, such as CCTV, the involvement of those who worked in the late night economy, particularly door supervisors through the formal door and club watch schemes, and the design of the entertainment areas themselves.

CCTV has been shown to be a useful tool in deterring crime (Brown, 1995; May et al., 2000) and is becoming increasingly a condition of the granting of Public Entertainment Licences. Both sites had CCTV covering the entertainment area and generally this was seen as useful in extending formal surveillance and in providing supporting evidence. In the event of criminal activity, the deterrent value of CCTV on licensed premises was questioned by officers. While many premises had systems, staff were rarely employed to monitor the screens on an ongoing basis and they were useful only after a crime had been committed. In addition the tapes used were often not of high enough quality to offer any real evidence. On the other hand, the city-centre systems monitored by the police were useful in spotting problems early and in tracking individuals/groups as they moved around the city-centre area. Linking this system to the pubwatch and radiolink systems which operated in both sites allowed the police to react to an incident more efficiently, with those using the systems alerting the CCTV operator to potential trouble as it occurred.

Door supervisors working in co-operation with the police were seen as an important element in the management of the entertainment areas of both sites. Only site 2 had a registered door supervisor scheme. The lack of a registered door scheme was a frustration in site 1, particularly for licensing staff, who believed that registration would deter less suitable applicants. Door supervisors had a mixed reputation, with officers having both good and bad experiences of them. Accusations of assaults by door supervisors (see Lister et al, 2000 for discussion) were an issue at both sites but were a particular problem in site 1. It is not only the police that have problems with door supervisors; it is also an issue for licensees:

I have experienced many many problems with doormen. Doormen are a major concern when you are trying to run a professional operation and especially trying to be a customer friendly operation ... try(ing) to maintain law and order and trying to find a doorman who is able to maintain law and order and do it in a professional manner is very difficult. (Licensee, Site 2)

Both police and licensees believed that the introduction of a national registration scheme was the best way forward to control the door supervisor industry (see Walker, 1999 for discussion). Key issues mentioned were the standardisation of training, freedom of movement for workers within the industry,[2] professionalisation of the job and creating additional qualifications to single out the better supervisors for key roles such as head door supervisor posts. The role of a well-trained and respected head door supervisor was seen by both police and licensees as pivotal in both creating and controlling the door team. Generally, door supervisors were perceived as useful and essential tools in policing the night time economy, particularly when linked via a radio system. Both sites had radio links in operation between the door supervisors and the police, and again this was seen locally as an extremely helpful tool.

The general design of the entertainment area and the licensed premises can help to alleviate potential problems. The use of toughened glassware, adequate seating, controlling numbers, and the physical design of the premises were all mentioned as useful in controlling the licensed environment. Licensees and police in both sites spoke of the problems caused by a lack of public transport (particularly taxis) and the congregation of crowds around a few fast food outlets (see Deehan, 1999 for further discussion).

Enforcement and the role of the licensing unit

One of the most common responses to any policing issue is to suggest more police officers on the street. Generally, the police officers agreed that this would help, particularly at night, to prevent incidents escalating. At both sites it would seem that weekend numbers could be low because of natural wastage – officers sick, deployed on other duties or on leave – and at times this could be particularly problematic. In the previous section, the need for female staff to perform particular tasks was highlighted. This could also exacerbate the situation when female officers are taken from regular duties to work in the custody suite – even for a short period of time. In these circumstances the role of and liaison with door supervisors becomes even more important. Both sites used special constables to boost their numbers on the street. The attitudes of police officers to 'specials' were mixed. Some felt they were of little practical use because their training and experience was not to the required standard while others felt they were a useful additional resource as another presence on the streets.

Both sites had a small licensing unit which dealt with the administration of licensing applications and collected intelligence (via the police crime recording systems). This intelligence was used to highlight which licensed premises might be

2   A national scheme for the registration and training of door supervisors, developed under the auspices of the Private Security Industry Act (2001), will not be fully operational until 2003. In the meantime, door staff wishing to work in more than one area of the country must re-register with each local registration scheme, and undergo the locally-run training courses and police checks.

having a problem with disorder. Both sites produced a list of such premises and then tasked the uniformed night shift to visit these premises on a weekend night without prior warning. While in theory this sounds useful, it does have certain key problems. Firstly, weekend nights may be very busy for a night shift responding to calls. As a result, some premises might not be visited and on particularly busy shifts no visit might be made. Secondly, officers expressed doubt about how seriously these visits were taken by the premises. Thirdly, there were questions raised about the training of the average officer to undertake the visits. In both sites the licensing unit tended to work day shifts and as such those with experience in the licensing laws generally did not make these calls unless there was a specific problem.[3] The staffing levels in both units made it very difficult for either licensing team to do such visits on a regular basis and both had a great deal of administration to deal with in terms of the processing of the licences themselves. So while the licensing staff did sometimes make night-time visits to problem premises most of these visits depended on the night shift team having the time to undertake these duties. Equally there was some criticism of how the tasking was communicated to the night shift team in Site 1:

3   Licensing staff in both sites made premise visits to all applicants.

> *The problems for Friday and Saturday nights, ask a sergeant to visit a premises but don't tell them what for…you have an idea but what else (to look for)…for instance serving to drunks…licensing officer not here now but what licensee finishes at 4pm. There is a lot of work that goes on during the day but there is also a lot to do in the evening. (Custody sergeant, Site 1)*

Both sites had a tiered approach to potential problem premises. The night shift visits were the first step. Both sites approached the licensee next (usually informally) followed by a meeting with the area manager and licensee if problems persisted. The process would then become more formal and could lead to licence revocation. The main theme running through the interviews with licensing staff was the importance of this relationship with local licensees. The police were keen to eradicate the belief that a licensee calling for police assistance would be a black mark against the premises. In fact the police suggested, it could work in their favour because it may be seen as an attempt to curb problems. Equally, many commented on the responsibility that lay with the licensee to employ professional door supervisors and to uphold the licensing law generally.

> *I think the licence trade could do an awful lot to help themselves. They obviously are committing an offence if they let people get drunk on their premises. I don't think the police deal with that, I don't think we have enough control over the licensed premises in the city-centre to do that. (Beat officer, Site 1)*

As one of the main roles of the licensing unit is to collate intelligence, the storage and access to information about licensed premises is clearly crucial. Only site 2 at the time of interview had a computerised licensing system. The site 1 licensing unit (which covered 600 premises) held paper files, stored in 12 filing cabinets, on every premises. These files were manually searched when intelligence was needed upon a particular premises. The computerised system at site 2 made the collation of reports on individual premises or areas of the city-centre a much less time-consuming job. In addition this system could be accessed for intelligence purposes by officers patrolling the city-centre who could also up-date files on the system as necessary.

4 *The White Paper 'Time for reform; Proposals for modernisation of the licensing laws' was published in April 2000.*

The proposed liberalisation of licensing hours [4] was greeted by the police and the licensees both positively and negatively. The police felt that staggered closing times would be useful in spreading the numbers of people on the street over the night and thus spreading the potential disorder problems over a longer period – avoiding the flash points they currently deal with:

> It will benefit us. I think that some people think that when the bell rings at 11pm they have got to get as much beer down their necks as fast as they can. If that bell never rings then there won't be a time pressure. They can spread their drinking over a longer period. Once people realise that they can get a drink whenever they like you don't have to be silly with it. (Custody sergeant, Site 1)

Equally, problems could be foreseen. Some officers believed that the predictability of the disorder they deal with currently made it manageable. This predictability would be lost in the new system. The licensees also saw the value in liberalisation but some suggested that it would not necessarily mean more business for them. Those who felt negatively about extending the licensing hours referred to the local drinking culture which they believed would not adapt well to extra time. Discounted drinks promotions were not seen as a problem in site 1 but several officers in site 2 referred to Monday nights as being a particular problem because it was a night traditionally aimed at students, targeting them with cheap alcohol.

Alleviating the problems in the custody suite

The use of camera cells
Site 1 had three camera cells which allowed vulnerable prisoners to be observed constantly, if necessary, from the custody desk. This was without doubt a very useful tool. At least on one occasion during the fieldwork a self-harm episode was prevented when an arrestee managed to secrete something into the cell despite being searched. While these cells did not eradicate the need to undertake physical checks they do provide an extra level of surveillance within a busy environment.

Site 2 custody staff felt they would improve working conditions given the physical problems of working in an old building. A few officers highlighted problems with the widespread use of cameras in cells including the lack of privacy, particularly for female arrestees. In addition some felt that cameras would simply be another target for an agitated arrestee.

Medically trained personnel in the custody suite

This study did not seek to establish the extent of medical knowledge amongst the officers interviewed. However, while all were first aid trained many had not had this training updated recently. The care of arrestees in custody is a major responsibility and several officers expressed the view that they were not well enough trained to do this work:

> A nurse in a hospital, she would have to have gone on a certain course to dish out these tablets on her own or if not there has to be two people. We are just giving out drugs just because a doctor says so ... and we are not medically trained., I mean that is daft, they are classed as class A and class B drugs. (Civilian detention officer, Site 1)

The potential for medically trained personnel to be located within the custody suite was welcomed by most officers who believed a presence in the suite (at peak times at least) would alleviate their fears. Dispensing drugs and the responsibility for the physical condition of the arrestee were sources of concern for staff. The main issue for interviewees was not the need for better trained medical personnel but who should be trained. Training police officers to a higher level was explored in the interviews and this was met with a mixed response. Some felt it would just produce more responsibility for officers with little compensation for taking on such responsibility:

> More responsibility on police officers…we are still not doctors. More responsibility with less training…would not be paid any extra would not get any incentive…anything that costs money is balked at. (Beat officer, Site 1)

Moreover, police officers do not tend to stay in one post for a long period of time, as such there would exist a necessity to retrain officers to a high standard on a regular basis. Consequently, putting resources into training of civilian personnel might reap more benefits, the strength being that civilian staff remain in the job for longer and have a narrower remit than police custody officers thus enabling them to focus more on health issues. The civilian personnel interviewed in site 1 had all served for several years in custody. Training either a police or civilian officer to this level would not be without costs, particularly financial costs in the short term. However, there are potential gains beyond the obvious in such training. One would expect an increase in confidence among custody staff having a medically trained member of staff available more often. Likewise, the frequency of the need to call out forensic medical examiners might be reduced, as would the waiting time for an FME to arrive. The level of training would then be an issue:

> I would hope that it would be at least paramedic standard, otherwise I don't think it would be worth it to be quite honest.... I could see some value of it, whether that value would be cost-effective with the cost of training them, the cost of keeping them updated with their training because obviously systems and procedures do change.(Licensing inspector, Site 1)

One has to question whether training custody staff to a paramedic standard is appropriate or whether the demand for this level of intervention can be justified financially. Would the employment of paramedics or nurses at peak times be more useful? Would it be better to ensure that all custody staff were up-to-date in their first aid training? Or would it be more useful to train a few officers to an advanced level so that their recognition of early problems is enhanced? These are all questions for potential investigation.

Potential for intervention

Without doubt those arrestees observed during this research represented a range of different types of drinkers; from those who have consumed too much alcohol on a particular occasion, to those who drink heavily on a regular basis to those who are suffering adverse effects from their drinking, to dependent drinkers. Hence, the custody suite may well represent an ideal setting within which to target a range of different types of drinkers with different levels of problems. It could offer an opportunity for preventative work with non-problematic drinkers or to divert problematic or dependent drinkers into the appropriate treatment services. The potential to deliver public health messages through leaflets given to arrestees as they leave the custody suite was discussed with officers. Few officers felt this would have much, if any, impact:

> I think the strike rate would be one in a hundred. Most don't even pick up their notification that they have been cautioned...I think the majority would bin it...(Custody sergeant, Site 1)

It was also felt that those regularly arrested while drunk would not respond to a leaflet and needed something more intensive. This pessimism is not without foundation as the early arrest referral schemes for drug users found this to be true (Edmunds, 1998).

The obvious next step could be to attempt to replicate in some way the drug arrest referral schemes for alcohol users. The main difference between a scheme for alcohol and one for drugs may well be that while the drug users referred into such schemes are usually dependent those arrested while drunk may not be. It should be remembered that most of those observed in this study were young drinkers. The appropriate intervention with such drinkers may not be as invasive or as time-consuming as for a dependent drug user. Such a scheme could offer public health education to drinkers to help reduce levels of drinking and prevent the escalation of consumption to problematic levels.

Both civilian and police staff felt that the custody suite could not be a suitable setting for any intervention given that those targeted would be likely to be intoxicated when entering custody. Few felt a non-mandatory intervention would be taken seriously if attempted when they were ready to be released. While officers (both police and civilian) showed an understanding of the different types of drinkers they came into contact with ('bingers' versus 'alcoholic'), most did not recognise the need to attempt to deliver a public health message to all drinkers. When interviewed about interventions most spoke of dependent drinkers rather than the young binge drinkers. This may be because there was a certain amount of sympathy for the Friday or Saturday night drunk and disorderly arrestee, but could also indicate a need for training. Though the custody suite at the time of arrestee release was not deemed a suitable setting, the issue of a delayed caution with an element of public health information was raised. This brought a mixed reaction. Some felt it would not work mainly because it would not be taken seriously. Others thought it would be best delivered at this point, when the arrestee had mentally processed what had happened to them and could therefore place any intervention within context:

> *It would be almost like they would be sentenced to a day...I think it would be a good idea...make them think twice rather than walk out of the station and think they have got away with it. Make them think about it in the cold light of day...I think that could have an effect on some people for minor offences. (Beat officer, Site 1)*

While officers could not necessarily see the value of offering public health messages in custody, they could see the value of education for the general population. There was a great deal of awareness of local drinking patterns and cultures – and most commented that it was that which needed to change before any real inroads could be made into the problem.

This culture in England is that you have a drink, you have a fight and you smash something – don't you. That is the culture unfortunately. I mean OK everybody has got their problems ..I mean I went to Paris for a weekend and we could sit outside and have a drink and there were no yobbos. It was nice. There is no way I would do that in site 1. (Civilian licensing officer, Site 2)

In particular most officers in site 2 described the 'circuit' drinking that took place at weekends. This involved groups meeting up in the same pub at the beginning of the evening and moving from pub to pub to club throughout the evening – consuming one or two drinks in each venue. The same route seemed to be taken on every night out – with the sole intention of getting drunk.

They're coming out to get blitzed, that's the top and bottom of it, and if they don't, if they go home and the next morning if they can remember what they were doing, they've had a bad night. They've come out with the sole intention of getting themselves smashed out of their mind. (Beat officer, site 2).

Alternative settings for 'drying out'
Custody staff were particularly concerned about the possibility of an arrestee dying while in their care. In terms of substance misuse deaths this concern is not without foundation: up to 25 per cent of the deaths in custody have been found to be related to either drug or alcohol use (Leigh et al., 1998). This begs the question whether intoxicated arrestees should be sobering up while in police custody when many of them need regular supervision during that time. More serious mental and physical illnesses can be mistaken for intoxication, which can also mask injuries or indeed other substance misuse.

When discussing alternative settings for the care of drunken arrestees several issues need to be addressed. Firstly, the drinking status of the individual, whether they are dependent drinkers, problematic drinkers or intoxicated to this level for the first time; who will assess their drinking behaviour; whether the purpose of the setting is to allow the individual to sober up, to offer an intervention or to divert into treatment; if the local treatment services are capable of dealing with the extra demand that such a setting might create; and if the numbers of drunken arrestees would make such a setting viable. There is, as yet, not enough information about the types of drinkers who come into contact with the police to enable these issues to be addressed.

5   *Arrests for drunk and incapable are usually made to protect the individual arrested.*

In the early 1980s, the Home Office undertook an evaluation of a detoxification centre in Birmingham (Kingsley and Mair, 1983). Only males arrested for being drunk and incapable[5] were sent to the centre. Most had severe alcohol, health and other social problems. The report acknowledged that while the centre worked well as a diversionary tool, the full potential of such a centre could not be achieved unless it was integrated into the network of local services. It also suggested that the frequency with which drunken arrests are made in any city-centre would mean that any such centre would be under-used. This study points to the amount of individuals arrested while drunk being significant (particularly at weekends), however most were arrested for more than simple drunkenness. Usually there was an element of disorder involved in the offence, hence all had the potential to remain within the Criminal Justice System. Consequently, the problem arising is that should they be taken to a detoxification centre to sober up they would still need to be released back into police custody to be charged or cautioned. In its capacity as a multi-agency body, the local Drug Action Team – if incorporating alcohol into its remit – could be in a position to facilitate working and arrangements for detoxification centres between health services and police. Few arrestees in the present study could be described as the typical 'habitual drunk' and were unlikely for the most part to have the health and other social problems of such individuals. However, they were drinking at the very least irresponsibly and as such would benefit from public health information in whatever way it was delivered. Any real consideration of alternative settings to care for this group of individuals would obviously need further research.

7. Conclusions

In this study, undertaken at pub and club closing times, almost six in ten arrestees displayed signs of intoxication and a significant proportion of these were aggressive, obstructive or non-compliant during custody procedures. Officers were often subjected to verbal – and at times physical – abuse and the custody suite was often a noisy and stressful environment to work in. Licensees also reported a range of problems associated with drunken individuals.

The findings highlight a number of areas where there may be potential for intervention to reduce disorderly and criminal behaviour in city-centre entertainment areas, to assist the work of the police, and to address the health risks presented by intoxicated arrestees. Key recommendations are outlined below, and fall into three categories:

- city-centre management

- deterrence and detection

- care and management in the custody suite.

City-centre management

There is a need for an holistic and integrated approach in the management of crime and disorder problems related to alcohol in the city-centre late at night.

- Addressing the problems requires a multi-agency approach, utilising the knowledge, skills and resources of the police and local licensing units, the local authority, treatment services and licensees. Such a multi-agency approach could be facilitated by the local Drug and Alcohol Action Team, Community Safety or Crime and Disorder Reduction Partnership. Strong links between the various stakeholders are crucial for the success of initiatives, not only because they foster good relations and thereby encourage positive action, but also because they facilitate the sharing of local intelligence.

- By their very nature, city-centre entertainment districts attract large numbers of people at one time who may compete for the same space, services or facilities. Problems are often concentrated in particular areas and it is important these are identified and measures taken to resolve them. For example, adequate transport should be provided to quickly disperse people at the end of the evening and there should be a sufficient number of fast-food outlets open. The staggering of closing times of licensed premises is also an initiative that may be effective.

Deterrence and detection

There is scope for the deterrence and prevention of criminal or disorderly behaviour in this context at the situational level.

- It is evident from the findings of this study that crime and disorder problems relating to alcohol and the night-time economy are largely predictable. The majority of incidents occur within a defined area of the city and at specific times of the day and week. Accordingly, high visibility policing can be targeted at the 'hotspots' at busy times. Whilst it is recognised that staffing levels at weekends can be low, there is potential for the better targeting of resources and deployment of staff at those times. CCTV is also being shown to be a useful tool in the deterrence and detection of criminal activity within the area covered and assists in the deployment of officers swiftly and appropriately.

- Local licensing units play a crucial role in enforcing licensing regulations. Whilst acknowledging the problems posed by limited resources, carefully targeted visits to licensed premises at busy times are recommended in order to ensure that laws are not being flouted, and prevent the potential for problems that may stem from poor serving or security practices.

- There are a number of ways in which the individual licensee can help to prevent incidents of crime and disorder occurring or escalating in and around their premises. Examples include the substitution of standard quality glass and bottles with toughened glass or plastic 'glasses', reduction of overcrowding or the potential for 'pinch' or 'flash' points by well-designed venue layouts and the implementation of well-advertised good serving and security practices. These could all be introduced relatively easily over time, if incorporated into glass replenishment orders, planned re-fits and with the training of new staff, respectively.

- Licensees can also assist policing of the city-centre by installing well-managed CCTV, ensuring bar and door staff are well-trained, employing good record-keeping practices, and by signing up to pub watch and club watch schemes that put different entertainment venues in direct contact with each other and the police.

Care and management in the custody suite

Detention in custody of intoxicated people presents a number issues relating to the safety and healthcare of those intoxicated arrestees.

- This report recommends the installation of closed circuit television cameras in certain cells, where they do not already exist, to enable the remote supervision of vulnerable detainees, including those who are intoxicated. Not only would this help to protect the health interests of the detainee but could also potentially overcome some of the logistical and resource issues relating to the need to make frequent checks of vulnerable detainees in their cells.

- Consideration should also be given to having medically trained personnel in the custody suite, at least at peak periods, to provide on-site care to arrestees in less serious condition and make informed decisions about the need for the presence of a doctor or transfer to hospital as appropriate. This could involve training custody staff, such as civilian custody officers, to a higher standard, or by employing a nurse to be present at busier times.

- Arrestees with alcohol problems, whether in terms of dependent or harmful drinking patterns, may be amenable to a brief health intervention while held in custody, whether administered by the FME or other medically trained personnel. Alternatively, arrestees could be screened for alcohol problems and referred to services as appropriate (similar to the drug misuse arrest referral schemes). Such interventions have the potential to reduce levels of 'risky' drinking patterns of the younger binge drinker and divert them from further alcohol-related criminal or disorderly behaviour.

- Greater consideration should also be given to the setting up and use of detoxification centres. Where detoxification centres have been piloted, only 'habitual' drunks arrested on simple drunkenness offences have been referred. However, if detoxification centres are to be considered as a viable option they could also consider taking other intoxicated detainees who may have been arrested for reasons other than simple drunkenness.

A final observation is that little research into what is effective in reducing the problems of alcohol-related crime has taken place in the UK, and the little that exists is at least ten years old (for example, Ramsay, 1982, 1989 and 1991; Tuck, 1982). Whilst it is clear from this that further research is required on what is effective at a national level, the necessary starting point for intervention and implementation of new strategies at the local level must be the evaluation of the tools and strategies already being employed locally.

Appendix A: Data collection schedule

**Home Office Policing the Late Night City-Centre Project
Alcohol-related crime and disorder**

CUSTODY NUMBER:

Section 1: Offence & offender information

Offender gender:	Male	[	]
	Female	[	]

Offender age:	Date of Birth		
	Under 18	[	]
	18-25	[	]
	26-35	[	]
	36-45	[	]
	46-55	[	]
	56+	[	]
	Not known	[	]

Ethnicity:	White	[	]
	Black	[	]
	Asian	[	]
	Other	[	]

Day and date of arrest: . . . .

Time of arrest: . . . .

Time of processing in custody suite: . . . .

Occupation . . . .

Offence arrested for: . . . .

. . . .

. . . .

Reason for arrest: . . . .

. . . .

. . . .

Where arrested?

Home	[	]
Pub	[	]
Club	[	]
Restaurant	[	]
Friend's house	[	]
Work	[	]
Other (state)		

Has alcohol been consumed in the 12 hours prior to your presence here?

Yes	[	]
No	[	]
Refused to answer	[	]
Unable to answer	[	]

Where has alcohol been consumed?

Home	[	]
Pub	[	]
Club	[	]
Restaurant	[	]
Friend's house	[	]
Work	[	]
Other (state)		

Remand decision:	Pre-charge bail	[	]
	Unconditional police bail	[	]
	Conditional police bail	[	]
	Remand in police custody	[	]
Exception to the right to bail:	Would fail to surrender	[	]
	Would commit further offences	[	]
	Would interfere with witnesses	[	]
	Either way/Indictable offence on bail	[	]
	Defendant's own protection	[	]
	S.7 Bail Act 1976	[	]
	Insufficient information	[	]
	Other (state)		
Grounds for decision:	Previous offences	[	]
	Previous bail record	[	]
	Community ties	[	
	Current offence/likely sentence	[	]
	Other (state)	[	]
Conditions attached to bail:	Not to contact X,Y, Z	[	]
	Residence	[	]
	Not to approach X,Y, Z	[	]
	Curfew	[	]
	Report to the police	[	]
	Surety/security	[	]
	Surrender passport	[	]
	Other (state)	[	]
Action taken:	Remand	[	]
	Cautioned for offence	[	]
	Charged with offence	[	]
	Not known	[	]
	Other (state)	[	]

Offence for which charged/cautioned: . . . .

. . . .

Does the prisoner ask to see the FME?   Yes   [   ]
                                          No   [   ]
                                          Not known   [   ]

Was the force FME called?   Yes   [   ]
                                          No   [   ]
                                          Not known   [   ]

Reason for calling the FME: . . . .

. . . .

Time of call to FME (if known): . . . .

Time of arrival of FME (if known): . . . .

Does the prisoner accept their right to see a solicitor?   Yes   [   ]
                                                             No   [   ]
                                                             Not known [   ]

Risk assessment (Potential for suicide/self-harm or illness while in custody):

Suffering from any illness?   Yes   [   ]   No [   ]   Not known [   ]

Medication?   Yes   [   ]   No [   ]   Not known [   ]

Previous attempted suicide?   Yes   [   ]   No [   ]   Not known [   ]

Previous self-harm?   Yes   [   ]   No [   ]   Not known [   ]

Section 2: Visible signs of alcohol intoxication

Does the researcher think the prisoner has consumed alcohol?   Yes   [   ]
                                                            No   [   ]
                                                            Not known [   ]

Does the researcher think the prisoner is drunk?   Yes   [   ]
                                                            No   [   ]
                                                            Not known [   ]

Is the arrestee:

Staggering?   Yes   [   ]   No [   ]   Not known [   ]

Sleepy?   Yes   [   ]   No [   ]   Not known [   ]

Slurring their speech?   Yes   [   ]   No [   ]   Not known [   ]

Smelling of alcohol?   Yes   [   ]   No [   ]   Not known [   ]

Other (state)

Section 3: Signs of drug misuse

Is there anything indicative of drug misuse?:

	Yes	No	Not known
Drugs found on arrestee(state which)	Yes [ ]	No [ ]	Not known [ ]
Small plastic bags found on arrestee	Yes [ ]	No [ ]	Not known [ ]
Rizlas found on arrestee	Yes [ ]	No [ ]	Not known [ ]
Silver foil found on arrestee	Yes [ ]	No [ ]	Not known [ ]
Swabs found on arrestee	Yes [ ]	No [ ]	Not known [ ]
Pipes found on arrestee	Yes [ ]	No [ ]	Not known [ ]
Rolled notes found on arrestee	Yes [ ]	No [ ]	Not known [ ]
Syringes found on arrestee	Yes [ ]	No [ ]	Not known [ ]
PNC check indicates drug use	Yes [ ]	No [ ]	Not known [ ]
Arrestee requests methadone	Yes [ ]	No [ ]	Not known [ ]
Arrestee claims to be a drug user	Yes [ ]	No [ ]	Not known [ ]

Other/s (state):

Section 4: Compliance with the custody process

Is the arrestee (tick relevant box):

Non-compliant   [   ]

Minorly compliant   [   ]

Semi-compliant   [   ]

Majorly compliant   [   ]

Fully compliant   [   ]

Fully compliant (but hostile)   [   ]

Section 5: Displays of verbal and physical aggression by arrestees during processing in the custody suite

Does the arrestee display/become involved in:

One-sided provocative behaviour   [   ]

Verbal arguments/disputes and threats   [   ]

Mild physical force or aggression   [   ]

Medium physical force or aggression   [   ]

Severe physical aggression and brawls   [   ]

None in custody suite   [   ]

(Code as many as relevant. Rank in order of progression i.e. 1 = state on arrival in custody, 2 = change in behaviour etc.)

Does the detainee need to be restrained?   Yes   [   ]   No [   ]

Appendix B: Tool for a multi-agency strategy to police city-centres late at night

Situational	Enforcement	Intervention
Local authority • CCTV • Town Planning • Public Entertainment Licence • Door Registration Schemes • Provision of transport	**Local authority** • CCTV • Regular Visits to Licensed Premises • Working with the Licensing Unit	**Local authority** • Liaison with police/treatment services/licensees re: local public health education
Police • CCTV • Liaison with Door Staff • Liaison with Licensees/Pub Watch • Liaison with Local Authority	**Police** • CCTV • More Officers • Regular Visits to Licensed Premises • Computer Package to Store Data on Incidents at Licensed Premises.	**Police** • Provision of public health information. • Liaison with local treatment services • Improved cautioning • Delayed-cautioning
Licensees • Ensure Quality of CCTV Tapes & Monitoring Procedures • Liaison with Police/Local Authority through Pub Watch • Design of Premises • Employ Trained Staff/Provision of Training • Employ Registered Door Staff	**Licensees** • CCTV • Ensuring Staff Refuse Service to intoxicated customers • Ensuring Door Staff Refuse Entrance to intoxicated customers • Refusing entrance to crowds of intoxicated men	**Treatment services** • Input into local crime and disorder partnerships • Liaison with police • Needs assessment of the type of drinkers passing through custody • Provision of appropriate public health information or intervention.

References

Bennett, T. (2000) *Drugs and Crime: The Results of the second developmental stage of the NEW-ADAM programme*. Home Office Research Study 204. London: Home Office Research and Statistics Directorate.

Brown, B. (1995) *CCTV in Town Centres: three case studies*. Crime Detection and Prevention Series Paper 68. London: Home Office.

Deehan, A. (1999) *Alcohol and crime: Taking stock*. Crime Reduction Series, Paper 3. London: Home Office.

Edmunds, M. (1998) *Arrest Referral: Emerging Lessons From Research*. Drugs Prevention Intiatives Paper 23. London, Home Office.

Graham, K., Wells, S. and West, P. (1997) 'A framework for applying explanations of alcohol-related aggression to naturally occurring aggressive behaviour', *Contemporary Drug Problems, 24*.

Hobbs, D., Lister, S., Hadfield, P., Winlow, S. and Hall, S. (2000) 'Receiving shadows: Governance and limitability in the night-time economy, **British Journal of Sociology**, 51(4), 701-717.

Homel, R., Tomsen, S. and Thommeny, J.L. (1991) 'The problem of violence in licensed premises: the Sydney Study', in T. Stockwell, E. Lang, and P. Rydon. (eds.) *The Licensed Drinking Environment: Current Research in Australia and New Zealand*, Melbourne, National Centre for Research into the Prevention of Drug Abuse.

Home Office (2000) *Time for reform; Proposals for modernisation of our licensing laws*. White Paper. London: HMSO.

Hope, T. (1985) 'Drinking and disorder in the city centre: A policy analysis', in *Implementing Crime Prevention Measures*, Home Office Research Study No. 86.London: HMSO

Jacobson, J. (1999) *Policing Drug Hot-Spots*. Police Research Series Paper 109. London: Home Office.

Kershaw, C., Budd, T., Kinshott, G., Mattinson, J., Mayhew, P. and Myhill, A. (2000) *The 2000 British Crime Survey, England and Wales*. Home Office Statistical Bulletin,18/00. London: Home Office.

Kingsley, S. and Mair, G. (1983) Diverting drunks from the Criminal Justice System. Research and Planning Unit Paper 21. London: Home Office.

Lang, E., and Rumbold, G. (1997) 'The effectiveness of community-based interventions to reduce violence in and around licensed premises: a comparison of three Australian models', *Contemporary Drug Problems*, Vol. 24, No. 4, 8-25.

Leigh, A., Johnson, G. and Ingram, A. (1998) *Deaths in Police Custody: Learning the Lessons*. Police Research Series, Paper 26. London: HMSO.

Lister, S., Hobbs, D., Hall, S. and Winlow, S. (2000) 'Violence in the night-time economy; Bouncers: the reporting, recording and prosecution of assaults' in *Policing and Society* (10) pp.383-402.

Marsh, P. and Fox Kibby, K. (1992) *Drinking and Public Disorder*. Oxford: Alden Press.

May, T, Harocopos, A. Turnbull, P.J. and Hough, M. (2000) *Serving Up: The Impact of Low Level Police Enforcement of Local Drug Markets*. Police Research Series Paper 133. London: Home Office.

MCM Research (1993) *Keeping the Peace: A Guide to the Prevention of Alcohol-related Disorder*. London: Portman Group.

Phillips, C and Brown, D. (1997) Observational studies in police custody areas: some methodological and ethical issues considered, in *Police and Society*, Vol 7, pp. 191-205.

Phillips, C. and Brown, D. (1998) *Entry into the Criminal Justice System: A Survey of Police Arrests and their Outcome*. Home Office Research Study Paper 185. London: Home Office.

Portman Group (1998) *Keeping the Peace*. London.

Purser, R.M. (1997) *Prevention approaches to alcohol related crime – a review of a community based initiative from a UK Midlands city*, Aquarius, Birmingham.

Ramsay, M. (1991) *Restricting public drinking: Studies by the Home Office and two Local Authorities*, Home Office Research Bulletin No. 30. London: Home Office.

REFERENCES

Ramsay, M. (1989) *Downtown Drinkers: The Perceptions and Fears of the Public in a City Centre*, Crime Prevention Unit Paper 19. London: HMSO.

Ramsay, M. (1982) *City Centre Crime; a Situational Approach to Prevention*, Research and Planning Unit Paper 10. London: Home Office.

Softley, P. with assistance of Brown, D. Forde, B. Mair, G. and Moxon, D. (1980) *Police Interrogation: an observational study in four police stations.* Home Office Research Study No. 77. London: HMSO.

Stockwell, T., Lang, E. and Rydon, P. (1993) 'High-risk drinking settings: The association of serving and promotional practices with harmful drinking', *Addiction*, Vol. 88(11), 1519-1526.

Tuck M. (1989) *Drinking and Disorder: A Study of Non-Metropolitan Violence.* Home Office Research Study, No. 108. London: HMSO.

Turning Point (1998) *An Evaluation of the Geelong Local Industry Accord.* Victoria: Alcohol and Drug Centre Inc.

Walker, A. (1999) *The Safer Doors Project*, Policing and Reducing Crime Unit, London: Home Office.

Policing and Reducing Crime Unit

Police Research Series papers

134. **For Love or Money: Pimps and the management of sex work.** Tiggey May, Alex Harocopos and Michael Hough. 2000.

135. **Reading between the Lines: An evaluation of the Scientific Content Analysis technique (SCAN).** Nicky Smith. 2001.

136. **Attitudes of People from Minority Ethnic Communities towards a Career in the Police Service.** Vanessa Stone and Rachel Tuffin. 2000.

137. **Assessing the Police Use of Decoy Vehicles.** Joanna Sallybanks. 2001.

138. **Widening Access: Improving police relations with hard to reach groups.** Trevor Jones and Tim Newburn. 2001.

139. **Risk Management of Sexual and Violent Offenders: The work of Public Protection Panels.** Mike Maguire, Hazel Kemshall, Lesley Noaks, Emma Wincup and Karen Sharpe. 2001.

140. **Risk Assessment and Management of Known Sexual and Violent Offenders: a review of current issues.** Hazel Kemshall. 2001.

141 & 142. Awaiting publication.

143. **In Sickness and in Health: Reducing sickness absence in the Police Service.** Jenny Arnott and Kaite Emmerson.2001.

144 & 145. Awaiting publication.

146 **The Role of the Forensic Medical Examiner with "Drunken Detainees" in Police Custody.** Alison Noble, David Best, Margaret Stark and E. Jane Marshall. 2002.

147. **Flexible Working Practices in the Police Service.** Rachel Tuffin with the assistance of Yasmine Baladi. 2001.

148. **Consultation by Crime and Disorder Partnerships.** Tim Newburn and Trevor Jones. 2002.

149. **Diary of a Police Officer.** PA Consulting Group. 2001.

151. **Crime and Disorder Reduction Partnerships: Round one progress.** Coretta Phillips, Jessica Jacobson, Rachel Prime, Matt Carter and Mary Considine. 2002.

152. **'Hard-to-Reach' Young People and Community Safety: A model for participatory research and consultation.** Rachel Pain, Peter Francis, Ingrid Fuller, Kate O'Brien and Sarah Williams. 2002. *Briefing note only. Full report to follow*

Crime Reduction Research Series papers

5. **RV Snapshot: UK policing and repeat victimisation**. Graham Farrell, Alan Edmunds, Louise Hobbs and Gloria Laycock. 2000.

6. **Not Rocket Science? Problem-solving and crime reduction**. Tim Read and Nick Tilley. 2000.

7. **Developing Crime Reduction Plans: Some examples from the Reducing Burglary Initiative.** Liz Curtin, Nick Tilley, Mark Owen and Ken Pease. 2001.

8. **Tackling Theft with the Market Reduction Approach.** Mike Sutton, Jacqueline Schneider and Sarah Hetherington. 2001.

9. **An Exploratory Evaluation of Restorative justice Schemes.** David Miers, Mike Maguire, Shelagh Goldie, Karen Sharpe, Chris Hale, Ann Netten, Steve Uglow, Katherine Doolin, Angela Hallam, Jill Enterkin and Tim Newburn. 2001.

10. **An International Review of Restorative Justice.** David Miers. 2001.

11. **Working out what to do: Evidence-based crime reduction.** Nick Tilley and Gloria Laycock. 2002.